T0077884

A^{The}rtPeace Project

PJ Keeley

WESTBOW
PRESS®
A DIVISION OF THOMAS NELSON
& ZONDERVAN

Scriptures marked WEB are taken from the THE WORLD ENGLISH BIBLE (WEB): WORLD ENGLISH BIBLE, public domain.

WestBow Press books may be ordered through booksellers or by contacting:

WestBow Press
A Division of Thomas Nelson & Zondervan
1663 Liberty Drive
Bloomington, IN 47403
www.westbowpress.com
1 (866) 928-1240

ISBN: 978-1-9736-0847-9 (sc)
ISBN: 978-1-9736-0846-2 (e)

Library of Congress Control Number: 2017918200

Print information available on the last page.

WestBow Press rev. date: 12/19/2017

I dedicate this book to my wife who taught me so much about caring for infants. And I dedicate this book to all those who care for babies! They are moms and dads, brothers and sisters, nannies, aunts and uncles, grandparents, neighbors, nana's, babushka's, and babysitters. Babies are helpless and need so much more than basic care. Your commitment to doing more can never be repaid. Doctors, nurses, medical techs, and anyone who protects or provides for our youngest humans: thanks to your caring, watchful eyes and dedication to the health and welfare of babies, from pre-pregnancy, prenatal, birthing, and beyond, our wonderful world of humankind will continue.

CHAPTER 1

---❦---

There is nothing like the laughter of a baby. A pudgy little human with a sense of humor will sit there until a sibling or parent comes along, and the tiniest movement or silly face can cause an eruption of laughter. Roaring, gut-level laughs will completely take over the baby, and the baby will focus all attention on you and react with continuous outbursts—sometimes until you are thoroughly exhausted.

Year-old babies are also a riot. A cousin of my wife had her almost-one-year-old at our first party on our new deck. They announced that he was about to walk any day. They gave him his push-train toy, and he was doing baby laps without any care about falling over the edge of the deck.

If Dad did not stop him and turn him around at every end of the road, he would have tumbled over an eight-inch drop.

After watching several hilarious laps with bright eyes, open mouth, and belly laughs, with Dad blocking every near calamity, I jumped up and announced, "We are going to get him walking today!" I looked into his smiling eyes, smiled myself, and moved in front of him. I talked to him and wriggled my fingers under his death grip on the handles of that toy. I got one finger into his left hand. He became alarmed as I detached that hand from the toy, and then I did the same for the other. He took hold of my fingers with the same death grip, and I didn't miss a beat. I began stomping like a cartoon character and gently led him around the deck. It was a funny dance. As I danced backward with short exaggerated footsteps, he followed and did his own stepping. He

1

was laughing, smiling, and began having just as much fun with me as with the toy.

After several laps, I laughed and said, "Now it is your turn to walk!" I continued our dance, but I wriggled my right finger out of the death grip of his left hand.

His face started to go white, and he stopped laughing.

I got his attention, and we continued dancing.

He was holding on with only one hand! I could feel his body sending all kinds of messages of danger as I tried to wriggle my other finger out. He increased his grip as I wriggled. We were able to go a few steps holding onto only one hand. I thought he would take those first steps on his own, but he collapsed into my arms in distress. He was so close! I held him, looked him right in the eyes, and said, "You almost did it! You can do it. Do you want to try all by yourself now?"

Without hesitation, his face turned very serious. He shook his head rapidly.

We all burst into laughter at his immediate and definitive "No!".

I am now, at age fifty-eight, comfortable enough to do the stunt I just described. However, until I became a father, I was ignorant of the many significant stages of growth of a child from birth to two years old.

Not until I was as an adult and faced with the challenges of being a provider did I even try to learn about caring for an infant. As a parent, I found myself having to crash-course learn all about a newborn, then a two-week-old, then a one-month-old, a six-month-old, and then a twelve-month-old. How could I have been so unprepared to care for a baby when my wife was capable of teaching others about the subject?

It is understandable that anyone facing parenthood unexpectedly and ill-prepared, male or female, would react the same as an almost-one-year-old when asked to do something on their own, which seems impossibly difficult and that they have never done before.

Having grown up with only brothers, my male-dominated household did not provide me with the experience of growing up with a sister who babysat. My mother always took care of my little brothers and shooed the boys out to play. We happily complied by vacating the area where the little screamers were. I cannot recall changing many diapers since my parents just did it all.

If my brothers or I babysat, the duty was similar to a prisoner's work party. We complied under threat of force because we could not get away. In my boyhood, I was quite settled on the concept that babysitting was wasting valuable outdoor sports activity time. I cannot recall many times when I came in contact with an infant for more than a minute or two. Maybe I would be told to acknowledge someone's new baby, but after completing our two minutes of forced compliance with plastic smiles, we were out on the ball field.

When my wife and I had our first child, my ignorance of all things baby hit me in the face like a big Lake Michigan wave, slapping me down as I tried to stand.

I could no longer shake my head and refuse to learn. I could not continue the way I always had before. The life of our child was at stake. I had to learn everything, and I had to learn it quickly! At that point, I became amazed and relieved at the incredible wisdom and baby-care experience that my wife already had. She provided me with a short list of things to do and when they needed to be done. Where did she learn all that she knew?

It was the craziest time of my life. I felt like I had discovered a new world full of babies and baby things. It was so different. It was a completely new way of living.

Babies are complex. Working with a baby can be an excruciating exercise for someone without great personal restraint, patience, or understanding.

Baby types are endless. There could be millions of different personalities that a baby might have. The baby's personality can be influenced by the mom, the dad, the environment, current conditions, preferences, and physical anomalies.

Babies are fragile. Caregivers must be aware of temperature, air quality, the roughness of cloth on a baby's skin, and more.

Babies require quick thinking. A person has to have great common sense and the ability to make fast judgments. Caregivers must be alert, aware of their surroundings, and cognizant of what food the baby is ingesting. What is touching the baby? What can come in contact with the baby? If a child is choking or coughing excessively, timing is important. There seemed to be an unending volume of things to be concerned about. Where did my wife gain this wealth of experience and knowledge?

Information was one thing, but real-life experience was a multidimensional teacher. In the same way some children grow up around a family business and become experts at an early age, caregivers get started at an early age when they have younger siblings. With girls in particular, this knowledge is provided and refined throughout many experiences. Aunts, grandmothers, and neighbors seem to be happy to share bits and pieces of information or even perform training on the spot.

This sharing of knowledge existed long before our computerized social media. This knowledge exchange resembles what our most advanced universities do: recording experiences, testing hypotheses, recording results, reporting findings, and educating others.

This informational data gained from many babysitting experiences is passed on to other babysitters who talk among themselves and filter out the principles of a particular task in the baby-care industry. One baby needs this, but another does not. This is good for a baby, and this is not. Do this to get them to sleep. This baby has a favorite toy. Don't lose this one's blanket. A young person immersed in the baby-care industry at an early age learns how to listen, organize, and prepare. As experiences and discussions continue, principles are developed and passed on. Wisdom is gained as young caregivers rapidly mature.

Babysitters can be highly tested at an early age. Some take on jobs for ten or twenty hours per week. Any craftsperson who has logged more than a thousand hours is usually considered an advanced producer. A high-performing sitter will attain local celebrity and can be overwhelmed by constant and numerous offers from the community to babysit. A great babysitter can be scheduled far in advance.

Girls who babysit are mini mama bears who take control of a top-level operation of paramount importance. They manage the lives of fragile children. Adults and peers embolden their courage. They develop an attitude of being able to handle anything that comes their way. The results are nothing less than outstanding. Within a few hours of each time a baby is watched over, a hundred disasters are avoided. The failures that do happen are relatively insignificant in the overwhelmingly successful babysitting episodes that occur billions of times daily all over the world.

Consider this: Adults hand over 100 percent control of the lives of their precious children to babysitters for several hours at a time, many times without a second thought.

Some people think that a woman experiencing an unplanned pregnancy would have a similar system to lead her to a positive, encouraging, uplifting end. She would be bathed in a chorus of positive words of wisdom from family members, neighbors, and society in general. Logically, it should be that way. In reality, it is not. The words that come from others who learn of an unplanned pregnancy are typically not positive. The words can be fearful, doubtful, uncertain, or even demeaning. There can be no words or an explosion of pent-up emotions with words that would never have been said without an unplanned pregnancy. Fathers-to-be run away, families can break apart, and support for the baby can disappear before the child arrives.

Imagine if I had spoken to that one-year-old about to walk and said, "You're not ready," "You can't do this alone," or "This isn't the time."

CHAPTER 2

---❖---

I n the past half century, a battle has been raging throughout humanity. The cause of the disagreement is the idea that someone's life can be decided upon in the womb. Women who feel that they are not ready for children or do not desire a child for other reasons might decide, after becoming pregnant, to end the pregnancy. Should each life be subjected to a choice—or is every life equal at creation?

There are social problems when there is a choice. If the choice of the future mother is not in agreement with the dad or other family members, should the father have any say in the matter? By law his wages can be garnished for child support if the pregnancy continues. If she is one way and he is the other choice, who gets to decide? What about grandparents, siblings, close friends, or relatives? Is their input of any value? Is the choice a woman makes always 100 percent yes or 100 percent no? Have women or men ever changed their minds on an issue? Does the growing fetus have any rights when choice is allowed? What does society have to do when choice is allowed by law? Should bars be directed to allow the serving of liquor to pregnant women who are scheduled to end a pregnancy? Is a pregnant woman who suffers an assault considered two persons or one? Would courts, police, and emergency medical personnel react differently if a woman states she is getting "choice" soon for her unborn child? Has a choice ever been made for a woman against her will due to a more physically or economically powerful family member, boyfriend, or life partner? Could a negative medical prediction about the future child's health be wrong? Has a dad ever wanted a child that a mother aborted? Has a woman who chose to abort ever regretted her decision?

With more than four decades of choice in the United States, we now have much experience with choice in the womb. There have been numerous problems, outrageous consequences, many disappointments, and injury-even death of women who desired choice from a clinic.

Does a pregnant woman have all the information she needs to make such a decision? Is the doctor at the clinic able to work fairly under the circumstances of the business in which he gets paid only if she aborts?

There has never been complete acceptance of the choice of abortion by a significant portion of US citizens. I am one of these citizens. Many years ago I discovered an organization called 40 Days for Life and I joined them.

40 Days for Life has grown to be the largest internationally coordinated pro-life mobilization in history, helping people in local communities end the injustice of abortion through prayer and fasting. Volunteers meet, organize and produce peaceful 40 day and night prayer vigil campaigns, now in over 300 countries. They also provide community outreach.

One time when I was praying on the sidewalk at the clinic, our abortionist drove up, rolled down his window, and sternly told me to keep away from blocking the front walk. Although I was not blocking, I moved even farther away immediately. I replied, "Yes, we want to follow the law." That seemed to surprise to him. He seemed a little shocked by my quick obedience. I have been constantly trained by our local Grand Rapids, Michigan 40 Days for Life board members to adhere to the rules of our peaceful prayer vigil, and I would never want to be the cause of a problem or worse, an arrest at one of our campaigns.

The next day, he pulled up again, but was much less gruff. Rolling down his window, he repeated his command of the day before. I was not blocking again. I moved even farther away and again replied, "Yes. We want to follow the law." My response seemed to amuse him. It was like he thought he could control me.

The next day, I put on my Tim Tebow New York Jets jersey. He was laughing at me as he drove in. He rolled down his window and jokingly said we needed to stay away from blocking the sidewalk.

I again responded, "Yes. We want to follow the law."

He apparently could not hear me or wanted to talk more to the buffoon wearing the Tebow jersey. He beckoned me to come closer.

I calmly stated, "Yes, I will move. We want to follow the law."

There was a slight pause. We exchanged looks, and time seemed to stop. He and I were so close at that time, yet we were so far away in our thinking. I got the feeling that he would enjoy going out with our pro-life team someday, that we would dine together and discuss all the years of our struggles against each other, and there would be many hugs and tears and bonding. A thought even passed quickly in my brain that he might be our next abortionist who would convert and become another superstar for life, like Dr. Bernard Nathanson.

In the quiet pause, I repeated, "We want to follow the law!"

He seemed to not have heard me the other days. I could see he was pleased we were not out to be combative, but there was another pause. I could not help but add, "Especially the law that states all mankind are created equal."

He immediately responded, "*Supposedly* created equal. Supposedly!"

I sensed he knew I would be happy to engage him on that discussion right there and then in front of everyone, but he rolled up his window to have the last word and drove away to go to work in his clinic.

Can a person who does not believe in the founding principle of the United States—that all mankind are created equal—be fair-minded when approached by a person in a crisis pregnancy situation?

Should a person who does not believe in the founding principle of the United States have any say in a matter in which he or she is paid if a life is taken?

CHAPTER 3

---❦---

History is a wonderful teacher. When the history of the abortion industry and the founding of our nation are examined, the following facts stand out. Two major icons of the choice industry changed their position from supporting and working to develop the industry to dedicating their lives to banning the practice from the planet. The founder's of the United States of America designed our government to protect individual freedom by making our most basic rights unalienable. Unalienable means we are never without our rights, they are endowed by our creator and therefore part of our anatomy, the same as having arms, or legs, or hair. No judge can remove them by the whim of someone else, including a parent or sibling or doctor or lawyer or judge.

Dr. Bernard Nathanson and Norma McCorvey (the Roe in Roe versus Wade) are both deceased now, but their message to anyone who will listen is vehemently pro-life. Of all people to have a voice in the matter, these two should be listened to most. Dr. Nathanson produced a video that can be seen on YouTube that shows how he became adamantly pro-life. His conversion came after he performed some ten thousand abortions and set up abortion clinics in the state of New York that were used as models for the industry. His video is factual and scientific. It is designed to convince those in the medical profession of his findings, and it is not recommended for the squeamish. Please do not show it to children. Many adults who have no medical background or training in surgery might find it painful to watch. His conversion is nothing less than amazing.

Norma McCorvey authored books and made videos, including a pro life commercial seen on national television in January of 2013. Her books are widely read and her public video messages also are on Youtube.

If Babe Ruth and Jackie Robinson had become anti-baseball, dedicating the remainder of their lives trying to end the sport of baseball, and many other baseball players were also leaving the sport forever, would the sports newscasters ignore it like our news ignores the number of former pro-choice proponents who are now pro-life?

Our nation was started on the premise of the value of an individual. The author of the Declaration of Independence was specifically creating a human rights document. I believe that our founder's intended that industries such as abortion should never be allowed. Our founders did not write documents that were difficult to understand or to which the meaning was not clear. We hold these truths to be self-evident would be written today as: We hold these facts to be captain obvious or, you don't need to check Wikipedia dude. Although there are thousands of historical writings over the last three hundred years of history of our nation, I ask you to consider the following, which pertain to the development of our founding document and defining principle of the USA, that all men are created equal.

Men means "mankind" and applies to all humans on the planet.

Thomas Jefferson lost a major court case in which he used the words born free (Howell vs Netherland 1770).

Jefferson lost the case because his opposing lawyer agreed that all are born free, but some are born free with a pre-existing condition. In this case, Netherland was providing food, clothing and shelter for the mother of Sam Howell, and she was Netherland's slave. Under British law, a person could be born free, but also born into slavery because of pre-existing conditions.

Thomas Jefferson was outraged at the ridiculousness of the laws of slavery, that would allow a baby to be born owing a debt.

A slave is a person who another can legally make choices for, regarding their life, liberty, and pursuit of happiness.

Thomas Jefferson authored the Declaration of Independence just a few years after his embarrassing loss in Howell vs Netherland and he specifically did *not* use the words born free.

Jefferson chose the words all men are created equal, which moves the timeframe from birth to creation when the person is in the womb of his or her mother.

Jefferson wanted all humans of all kinds to have the ability to be free and not have others make a choice for them regarding life, liberty or the pursuit of happiness.

The Declaration was edited and approved by Benjamin Franklin and John Adams, and it was reviewed and signed by all thirteen colonies who joined the rebellion of 1776.

By using the words created equal instead of born free, he removed the ability for someone to be born royal, and others to be born slaves.

By stating that all are endowed by their Creator with *certain unalienable rights*, that among these are life, liberty and the pursuit of happiness, Jefferson planted your rights into your being and made them unavailable for discussion or deletion by the courts. No one can take them away without severe cause.

Jefferson made government accountable to the people to protect individual rights and the right he mentions first and foremost is the right to life.

Although our founding document was written to be easy to understand, four score and seven years later, it took a civil war to settle the subject of slavery.

With over forty years of abortion in the USA, our debate on this issue has reached civil war proportions.

At the risk of inflaming a reader, but with the hope that this issue could be able to be resolved peacefully and with simple honesty and scholarly debate, I ask you to please pretend that you are a supreme court justice and answer this question. How is abortion allowable under the Declaration of Independence?

CHAPTER 4

❧

I grew up with the idea that there is a human life created at conception. I have always considered that common sense says that a pregnant woman has a small person growing inside her. I was taught that this life inside a woman is subject to protection under United States law, spelled out in our founding principle of the United States of America, which was declared in July 1776. When I found out I was in an unplanned pregnancy with my wife—and she was not my wife when we found out—I rallied to the forefront of the situation, to commit to the needs of my future family, without any real hard experience or practical skills in parenting to fall upon.

I have been learning about fatherhood ever since. Am I a proponent? Absolutely! I highly recommend fatherhood to each and every male on the planet. I could never have imagined what would happen in the next thirty years, but I would not trade those life events for anything today—good or bad. I am looking forward to the next thirty years, hopefully, and seeing my adult children grow and have families of their own.

Since I have the experience of participating in an unplanned pregnancy, I also have experience in handling the situation. I had an upbringing that is likely different from many others with this experience today. As a child, I had little television and no Internet. Throughout society, there was no legal option other than adoption. It was simple. There was no choice.

I did not have to deal with the incredible thought process women and men are asked to deal with in our advanced society.

I can only imagine that situations have arisen in which a woman would inform a man of his impending fatherhood, but he and she were only together in a casual manner and were not expecting to be attached to each other. Thus, the next discussion would involve what to do next. If he so desires, she and he could continue the process and live happily ever after.

Of course, that means that both would be dropping everything they are doing because the time to decide is right now—today. This kind of discussion is a recipe for disaster. I cannot say that it has been easy for me, because I did drop everything—and so did my wife. We proceeded to build a family.

When I was first informed, I did not hesitate for a second. I never considered that I had a choice. I did not want a choice in the matter. After she alerted me that she was pregnant, I thought about my child and told her that we needed to get married. I had little to no idea what I was doing. Thirty-three years later, I cannot believe the joy I have experienced. And that joy continues each day.

I have joy—not happiness. Happiness is like a flower that is beautiful for a short time, but you have to perform special care for it constantly. You only experience it for the time it blooms. For all of the happiness a beautiful flower brings, including its fragrance and beauty, it is fragile and wilts in the sun. It does not endure.

Joy is like an oak tree that grows and becomes stronger and taller. It will combat the blistering sun and provide relief with its shade. The oak tree grows and stands on its own as a solid component of nature. It has a certain niche in the world and provides places for birds to nest and acorns for squirrels to eat. The adult oak tree is like a castle reigning over an area of dominion, a small kingdom. When an oak is cut down, it takes a great amount of work to conquer it. Even after it is cut down and sawed into pieces, it continues to be an important asset by providing materials for creating heat or building a home.

My message to future parents is this: When an unplanned pregnancy happens, you should not concern yourself with your happiness at that moment. Consider the joy you will have forever. The years go by quickly, and what has been started by God and you can become a joy for all eternity.

To help you make this decision, the last part of this book contains many of the wonderful testimonies and stories about parenthood garnered during the most successful of all our campaigns: ThumbsUpGR. Please feel free to go to section two right away.

The ArtPeace Project was developed over several years and my journey was nothing short of amazing, and I hope you enjoy the next chapters. Throughout the years and the different campaigns, I prayed for guidance. I listened. I followed a path of obedience to God, but I was not so obedient! I encountered much difficulty, sadness, and joy. It is almost certain that if your tongue is used to praise Jesus in public, there will likely be someone nearby who will swing a two-by-four into your skull or harm you in some way—even your own family. The Bible warned us of this in Matthew 10:22: "You will be hated by everyone because of me, but the one who stands firm to the end will be saved."

Was Mary provided a palace with servants to handle the birth of Jesus? Were not government agents sent to eliminate Jesus as a baby, requiring Mary and Joseph to flee their home and country?

I pray that you find hope, peace, and solace in your decision making and your quest to serve. I thank God for all his blessings on my family and me. I praise God, the Father of us all, who sent his Son, Jesus, to us to proclaim the good news. At the cross, Jesus gave us His Mother, Mary, to be our shining example of faith. After Jesus ascended into heaven, He sent the Holy Spirit for our daily utilization in everything we do.

CHAPTER 5

---❖---

We were praying at an abortion clinic in 2010. I was on the sidewalk during the 40 Days for Life prayer vigil in Grand Rapids, Michigan. Our vigil was happening at the same time as our town's newest worldwide event, ArtPrize, which attracted some 300,000 visitors that year. As we stood silently praying, some passersby walked up to me and asked, "Where is the art here?" They were visiting from out of town and assumed we were there because of art. Because there was no ArtPrize sign informing them that this was an ArtPrize venue to explore, they decided to ask.

I said, "There is no art here. We are praying, and this is an abortion clinic."

This stunned them, and they left. I believe it was a strange feeling for them and certainly was for me. Neither of us was at ease to continue our conversation. They were in entertainment mode and going to a street party to join in all the fun. We were standing on the front lines of a battlefield over human rights, and we were deadly serious in our hope that the other side would succumb.

Something had to be done. Grand Rapids was a bright fire burning a hole in digital maps of travel agents worldwide as they searched for great places to visit, vacation, or have business meetings. Our new ArtPrize event—where our formerly humble city invites artists from anywhere and everywhere to exhibit their best work in our community—is breaking attendance records yearly. For several weeks, an army of diverse visitors become like little children on a playground as they mix, mingle, ooh, and ah while crossing bridges, wandering into buildings, and searching for the next art treasure. And a craft-beer restaurant was never more than a walk away.

With more than 1,500 artists baring their souls with their special creations for all to admire or criticize, ArtPrize was immediately a hit. It solved the problem travel agents had of finding the newest, hottest place, and it provided a super-friendly, welcoming community a reason to host a giant street party.

For 40 Days for Life, it was also a worldwide event. For forty days and forty nights, hundreds of towns worldwide hold prayer vigils at a site of atrocity to pray for the end of abortion. Quietly and vigilantly, thousands participate in the spring and fall each year, causing millions to think. Several thousand lives are saved from being "processed" with reproductive health care.

How could these two events happen at the same time in Grand Rapids? The media in Grand Rapids, like elsewhere, reacted to the organized prayer campaigns in a biased manner. By ignoring the 40 Days for Life campaign, they pretended they did not know about it, that it was not news, or that it did not matter. More than thirty churches of different denominations, nationalities, and creeds—representing more than a quarter of the population of Kent County—joined together to call attention to a medical practice that violates a founding principle of the United States.

It was extremely difficult to get people to give up their time and ask them to go stand outside a clinic where an unthinkable activity was happening and then ask them to pray in public. Many did, and I applaud and congratulate them. The majority of those opposed to abortion found that it was quite a lot to ask. Many young people could not attend. There were parking issues. It was not fun to be there. Many adults confessed that it was just not for them. There is a local political problem regarding a famous person from our city.

Grand Rapids was the town of Gerald R. Ford and his wife, Betty. Although President Ford was solidly pro-life, Betty was a major force from 1973 on—along with numerous popular singers and actors—for the cause of women's reproductive rights. This is a nice way to describe the taking of the life of an innocent, growing human being inside the womb. Betty inspired many women and worked tirelessly for women's rights, and Grand Rapids loves the Ford Family, as do I. As this book is compiled, a battleship has been christened for our former president. To be pro life in this town is almost to be against one of Betty Ford's favorite political victories, the introduction of abortion in 1973.

ArtPrize could only distract from our work to publicize the abortion clinic. With media focused rightly on a popular event, our efforts to get our message out would be eclipsed. The pro-choice leaning media simply ignored our peaceful and quiet protest.

CHAPTER 6

꧁

Our fall 2011 vigil had been scheduled for a herculean twenty-four hours each day for forty consecutive days. We were not filling each time slot. Sometimes an entire twenty-four hours of shifts would have only one person there to pray. Because I worked a late shift, I would take the 1:00 a.m. to 3:00 a.m. shift, sometimes every day of the week, just to fill in the time slot so that it was not left open. This effort seemed out of proportion compared to the results. I could get many prayers said in two hours, namely all four mysteries of the Catholic rosary. I got to view the sky with slow, swirling clouds and watch the moon and stars drift across the skyline of Grand Rapids. I did experience a quiet Fulton Avenue, which had thousands of cars traveling on it during the day. It was a treat to have a large American flag flapping in the nighttime breezes on each side of the clinic. I had to learn to never be totally unaware of bicyclists, even at late hours. They whizzed down the hill, within inches of me, while I was looking the other way. They did not warn me as they passed. When I jumped, they were already past me, which I suppose is safer than warning me causing me to move the wrong way. I learned that a skunk lived nearby and would come out to forage around the clinic at that time.

That beyond-the-call-of-duty effort on the sidewalk led to me getting angry at God. I would inevitably boil over after standing there for a while. I would look up and directly charge God with indifference. "How can you allow this?" I would silently scream. "How can you permit this violation of human rights to exist in our Christian and humane and kind city?" At that time of night, I felt like I had an uninterrupted, direct communication line to heaven and that God would hear my every complaint.

After those angry thoughts, I would soon overcome my emotions. I often received messages. Whether it was just a calming of myself or thinking about an idea, I began to contemplate ways to be more effective at changing the way things were in my city. As community-involvement chairperson for 40 Days for Life, and the life events coordinator for my Knights of Columbus council, I thought about how to get out a message of life and involve more people in our cause.

Our statistics on the sidewalk were dreadful. We could go weeks without changing anyone's mind. In Grand Rapids, thanks to the closing of the Muskegon clinic, two clinics in Lansing, and the other one in Grand Rapids, the clinic on Fulton Avenue became a sole supplier and quite a good moneymaker. To give you an idea of how bad our statistics are, if we got nine saves in the year, which was good for us—we probably lost 991, making our batting average a measly .009.

In ten years, 40 Days for Life—with campaigns in more than three hundred cities—could not claim more than twenty thousand lives saved. In the same time, upward of fifteen million abortions happened, which means less than 1 percent of women with children in the womb who headed to a clinic would change their minds because of 40 Days for Life. We were a big bunch of losers.

I was taking classes at the community college on Ransom, just north of Fulton Road, when I overheard a conversation in the library. It went something like this: "What? Really? Oh, don't worry. I know just what to do. I will get you an appointment at the clinic. It is right on Fulton. Yes. Don't worry. We will take care of this. No one has to know. No! Don't tell him or your parents. We will just go there. They have helped many women with the same problem. You will be all right! I will even take you there myself. Don't worry! Everything will be fine. I will call you tomorrow."

I did nothing that day, but I could not help but think about that girl. What if she called a friend who was pro-life? Instead of being led to a clinic, a pro-life friend might encourage her and build her up. What if she read about other unplanned pregnancies where it worked out to raise the child?

In 2016, in Battle Creek, Michigan, a young woman died after she went for an abortion. At the same time, an airline worker bumped a passenger. There was only a slight injury, but he was removed from the workplace. Eight months after the death of the young woman in Battle Creek, the responsible doctor was still practicing, the clinic was still open, the government rallied to protect the doctor, and the medical examiner provided a heavily redacted autopsy report.

There are many examples of how the abortion industry in Michigan was not concerned about the health of the pregnant woman, including the reinstatement of a doctor with a criminal past after verified complaints and convictions. A state official overrode his formal complaint to allow him to continue to practice.[1] That was accomplished with the full approval of legislators in the Michigan Senate and Congress who loudly proclaim their concern for women. These legislators are in office today and are proud to tell you that they did this.

I resolved to do something to educate the public, to expose the abortion industry for what it is. I desired not to do anything that was harsh, cruel, or combative. I believe that people are ill informed or have been told lies so long they accept them as truth. I am against the causing of grief, shock, or uneasiness, as I believe those methods are completely ineffective. The worst methods of

---

[1] Dr. Robert Alexander lost his license to practice medicine in 1990. Dr. George Shade, an official from the State of Michigan decided not to investigate the complaint, and Dr. Alexander was able to practice again in Muskegon. More complaints were filed, more patients were injured, and his dirty clinic closed due to a number of violations.

protest in the abortion fight used religion and personal attacks. The prayer vigil did not attack, but it did not attract.

I thought, *Why not present the pro-life message in a positive and fun, interactive, happy, and nonjudgmental way?*

CHAPTER 7

O ur home at that time featured cedar siding. On the front porch, water and ice had contrived a moldy residue around the water meter, and the deteriorated wood needed to be replaced. After six months of putting off the job, I finally decided to take on what looked like a ten-minute, less-than-twenty-dollar repair that my wife has been telling me about for longer than I care to admit. That fix cost over two hundred bucks as, not one, but many boards needed replacing, and I damaged the water meter in the process, which added a three-week wait to have water department approve the repair. After the ordeal was over, I kept the extra cedar boards and vowed to use every last piece of that wood for something.

It was my angst over this wasted wood expense that spawned my idea of how to promote life in a new way. What if instead of trying to get people to travel to a clinic to pray in public, where anyone would be uncomfortable, we provided an opportunity to create art with a pro-life message that we could display somewhere? We could involve youth and focus their attention on giving a positive message to a person in a tough situation. If we could involve schools, teachers could be in their own environment and integrate our project into their curriculums. Students could be asked to create pro-life art pieces. It seemed like a great idea.

I was expected to create events that involved youth per my church's men's group. In my pro-life experience, I saw the need to teach about this difficult subject at the earliest chance. I volunteered to do community outreach as my involvement with the 40 Days for Life campaign.

I thought about how much fun it is to create with paint. *How many students would want to make art if they had a contest? Many. What if I ask participants to make art to promote the peace that only Jesus can give?* I came up with the ArtPeace Project. I made several sample art pieces and thought about how it could be promoted to area schools. Over a few weeks, I set up a rough plan for how to get students to make pro-life art that we could display during ArtPrize. I explained the program to my wife—a teacher and my expert consultant on anything I wanted to do. As with anyone who has ever had what they consider a good idea, my first expectation in telling another was that they would also see my wonderful concept and encourage me!

Wrong. There were plenty of projects around the house that I could be working on that made more sense to do than trying to solve worldwide issues that could not be solved by one person by having kids making art. Even worse, in public schools, political issues such as the pro-life message are not allowed. A public educator who espouses one political issue over another in the classroom can be removed. This idea, regardless of how much I wanted it to happen, was dead in the water. It was a waste of time to even consider one more minute of trying to get it going.

However, I had already considered doing nothing. Doing nothing was what many were already doing. The choice message has been implemented and is taught at public schools. Children are being told they can get surgery, not just a bandage or an aspirin, *they can get surgery without the knowledge of their parents*, and a tax-payer funded organization would help them keep a surgical operation secret from the adults in their lives. This organization would even commit to forever keeping this surgery secret.

Upon further investigation of this tax-funded organization, I found that they were promoting sexual activity outside of marriage to teenagers via their website, and they would provide contraceptives, regardless of the fact that sexually transmitted diseases have skyrocketed amongst teens since they have been doing this.

This organization promotes itself as helping women. They provide abortions to any clients who accepted their free contraceptives and still got pregnant. They provide drugs to teenagers that kill cells inside the body. They are happy to use taxpayer funds to cover their fees.

This organization can be seen on campuses throughout the United States. Candidates for public office proudly announce that they support everything that the organization does.

In conversations with young people, I find that many have a perception of an abortion clinic that is a fairy tale. Their idea of the clinic is that it is pristine and clean, and highly trained professionals follow proper medical procedures while caring for each and every patient. They seem starry-eyed in their defense of these clinics. I am greeted with closed eyes and head-shaking disbelief when I report on my actual visits. I have seen the bloodstained surgery areas where blood from the last several years and hundreds of patients has never been cleaned. I have worked to remove former convicts who are performing surgeries on children without telling any adult responsible for that child. Certainly you would expect a government-approved medical facility would follow basic cleanliness and not be filthier than the worst gas station restroom, but the abortion clinics do not have to follow standard cleanliness procedures.

The abortion industry is a business. It has little to do with health care.

I decided to continue.

I set up a meeting to sell my campaign to the Grand Rapids 40 Days for Life. I was very confident. To my dismay, my first discussions were completely rejected. The 40 Days for Life board members were all volunteers who worked with about a two hundred-dollar budget. They did all their meetings on their own time and paid for all their expenses and gas. Their reaction to my plan was grim. They pointed out that I would be working on an art project with no predictable benefits. Any money that was needed was not available. In addition, it would distract from their already near-impossible tasks of coordinating the activities of thirty five churches. It could even derail those efforts, which were extremely vital and necessary. Encouraging me was completely out of the question.

That reaction was not what I expected at all.

I was sure that the ArtPeace Project was a winner, so I took the idea to my Knights of Columbus council. Surely I would find the welcoming enthusiasm that this idea deserves.

They were happy to listen—but quick to discourage any fundraising for it. A number of concerns were brought up. I found myself in a discussion about power. Who needs to be in charge? Our local council? That was not the right place.

I was referred to the state of Michigan council or even the supreme council of the Knights of Columbus. They handled large-scale operations like this. Another negative was the ongoing child molestation scandal of the Catholic Church. Our council was concerned about any activities involving youth since we were being monitored, and all Catholic organizations were subject to new requirements for working with youth. Two adults had to be in any enclosed area when a young person was around. Because it was a new idea, there was no budget, and it would take away from our already large commitment to existing projects, I was implored to help more with our current workload.

They said, "Your time would be better utilized on existing, approved, and well-known events rather than introducing a new project that could overwhelm us and cost way to much to run—all for a doubtful result."

Hmm. I had to retreat into myself and seek an answer to a difficult situation. I had to decide what to do. If I continued, I would be almost on my own. It could be very costly. I would lose the support of 40 Days for Life, the Knights of Columbus, friends, relatives, neighbors, my own kids, and my wife. *This work might be costly indeed.*

As I thought and prayed about whether I should continue, an event came to the front of my mind. In 2009, the 40 Days for Life campaign had no one to pray for any shift on Monday, October 12. I had the day off. October 12 is my mother's birthday. I decided to go and pray for the entire day, fulfill each of the six empty time slots, and then dedicate the effort to my mother. What a wonderful idea. I told God in my prayers that I would do it.

As the weekend approached, I performed about ten hours of overtime—along with working on the house, dealing with kids in sports, and I was exhausted. I began to consider all the effort I was expending for the cause. *I am doing a lot already. This day long effort is not as big a deal on the grand scheme of things.* I changed my mind. I decided on Sunday night that it was not that important. *After all, no ones else cares. I have so many things to do and really need to get some sleep.*

I changed my plans at the last minute and turned off my alarm.

I didn't hear my wife leave at five thirty to get to school to prepare for the two hundred high school students she dealt with each day. At six, my cell phone rang. My wife was desperate and talking fast. She had forgotten her laptop, and it had all the items she needed for whatever she was doing that day.

"No problem," I said. "I will get up immediately and bring it there right now."

She hung up, and I got up. I realized that I was going to be up at that time before I changed my mind. The abortion clinic was only ten minutes farther than the school. *Okay, God. I got the message!*

I reluctantly dressed for a boring day of being by myself on a busy street with people driving by, shouting slurs, accelerating, and all the derogatory shouts of "Get a life!" that accompany anyone who silently stands up for the innocent unborn. *I most surely will be the only one there.*

After I delivered her computer, I drove downtown and parked near the clinic. I made the long walk to the sidewalk. I was in the dark loneliness of Fulton Avenue at seven o'clock in October on a brisk thirty-degree morning. At least there was no rain. I decided to move about as I prayed. I walked west and then back to the east. When I walked east, I was going uphill at a thirty-degree rise. Ten minutes into my vigil, I felt very embarrassed that God had to prod me to do what I promised Him I would do. *Oh, how quickly we can fail after we take an oath or swear that we will do some service for God, become a good person, or stop sinning.*

I was thinking about how easily I had changed my mind. I tried to ignore the cars whizzing by. As I turned to the east, I ducked as an earth-shattering, metal-clanging explosion of sound came at me from behind! I thought it was a plane crashing on the road behind me, and then I thought it was an earthquake or building tipping over. Admittedly, when you are feeling remorse from the realization that you lied to God and you failed to make a wonderful statement to your cause—not to mention failing to create a wonderful birthday memorial for your very own life-giving mother—you are a bit sensitive to earth-shattering noises of any sort.

I quickly turned to see what was causing the noise. I saw a garbage truck with its engine revving full blast to get up the hill, and I heard the metal clanking vibrations from its numerous parts. I was still shaking from my first impression that the world was opening up to swallow buildings. I could do nothing but stare at it. Its massive engine and gear-changing noises continued as it tanked up Fulton road, and then it swerved into the driveway, bumping and clanging to the back of the abortion clinic.

I was completely at a standstill. I watched that massive metal box on giant tires roll down to the back of the lot. I hear the pneumatic pops as the monster forks plunged into the dumpster and then the screech of the lifting mechanisms as the huge steel container is raised and turned. I heard the swishing of items sliding into its steel belly, several bangs, and a final thud as the container was returned to the ground. The huge vehicle revs up and returns up the driveway and then banging and clanging turned onto Fulton.

As it passed me, I read the sign on the vehicle: "Medical Waste."

I was stunned and overwhelmed with emotion. As I realized what was inside that vehicle, I could not bear the thought or watch anymore. I fell to the ground, and tears flowed uncontrollably down my face. *Am I here as the only person attending the funeral of those children? They lose their lives and then are tossed away like trash? No obituary, no funeral, no anything. It was like they did not even exist.*

I promised God I would not let him down again! I would never stop fighting until that barbaric practice was ended once and for all. Could I give up and end the art project idea after that? I submerged into prayer, asked for guidance through the rough waters, and headed into the storm.

CHAPTER 8

I returned to my Knights of Columbus. Our grand knight, the guy tasked with making executive decisions, agreed to test it on a small scale—just at our church. If we got participation, maybe we would expand. I was thrilled to have a win, any win at that point, and I jumped in.

I believed I had a good starting plan. We would announce that we were accepting art and sell kits to parents with instructions for how to create a pro-life art piece. We would need participants to return the art within three weeks. I went to the garage and cut the cedar boards into eight-by-eight-inch square tiles. Each participant would have the same size base to work on. They would have to supply paint and any other materials. I would allow them to paint it or to make a sculpture. I decided a height restriction of seven inches would be necessary for sculptures.

It was a very hard sell. It was nearly impossible. We were not getting participants. The experiment was negative. Not one volunteered to produce art.

I was so disappointed that I did not know how to continue or if it even made sense. Worse, what if the pro-life art campaign was not meant to happen? As I left for work the next day, I was depressed and felt defeated. I succumbed to all kinds of negative thoughts—even those that proposed that maybe the abortionists were correct, that our concern over the welfare of infants in the womb was blown out of proportion, and that our concerns for the lives of the unborn were not what God wanted us to be concerned about. It was a low feeling.

The next day, I was working at my retention position in a cable call center. We had cable TV on in various places around the building on large screens. Regular programming was being interrupted by a news story about a shooting with injuries. The reporters were in disaster mode, trying to cover every detail in the event as it was happening. There was an all-out alert. An active gunman was on the loose, and several people had been shot.

As I watched, I realized it was happening very close by. The gunman was being pursued. The news people were issuing warnings to stay away from the area, but if you were there, be alert, take cover! The gunman was headed toward our call center. The reporters were anxiously trying to relay details and issuing warnings to take cover.

I was on a break, and I hurried outside to witness a low-flying police helicopter that was moving in circles and slowly progressing toward my building. I pointed it out to a coworker who had spent many years in the military. I said, "Hey, Fern. Do you have a gun in your car?" I was not calm.

We watched the activity in the sky and went back to the TV. They were actively warning everyone in the area to take cover. As we headed back to work, the reporters stated that there was only one gunman. He was surrounded in a residential area that was about three miles from us. The standoff was still happening when we headed home. It ended when the shooter committed suicide. He had killed several people. The dead were all family members, and they included young and old. Many people knew the family. The reports were heartbreaking. It was the largest mass murder in the history of Grand Rapids.

The very next day, another death was in our news. It was the passing of former First Lady Betty Ford. It was no small bit of news. Grand Rapids had been preparing for a stately funeral to honor her for many years.

In 2006, her husband died the day after Christmas. The town received national attention during a week of ceremonies.

Dignitaries from around the world flew in for the funeral. It was amazing how many people came to town that winter to stand along the roadways to say good-bye. The stories of his life were discussed nightly. All the branches of the military honored the former commander in chief. There was a YouTube video of air force fighter jets performing the missing man formation over the four hundred-foot-wide Grand River. The longtime public servant from Grand Rapids was showered with accolades, honors, and reports from hundreds he had worked with. It was a fitting tribute to a humble man who occupied the highest office of our government.

The media had prepared similar tributes to honor Betty upon her passing. However, the story about the mass murderer grabbed all the news coverage that week. There was nothing anyone could do. Who could have predicted such a sequence of events? The timing was horrible. Our former first lady was being eulogized all week, but the news could not ignore a shocking mass murder. It was very painful to have our former First Lady's funeral not be the top story. It got worse. The murderer's burial was the same day as Betty Ford's. The family of the murderer was approached and agreed to move the burial to another day. Could it be divine justice?

For more than forty years, the media has worked tirelessly to twist the truth about the abortion industry. Pro-life speakers were called "anti-choice." Abortion was renamed "health care," "reproductive rights," and "choice." If you opposed abortion, you were labeled anti-women. The media have created an image of abortion that seems to be righteous, legal, and necessary. But the news during the funeral of one of the founding icons of the pro-choice and pro-abortion industry could not be controlled. The woman who promoted abortion, which in truth was the destruction of a family member, shared the headlines during her funeral with a murderer who destroyed seven family members.

I collected the newspapers from that week and pointed out this seemingly obvious coincidence. I was delivering a donation from our men's group to a local pro-life ministry for young mothers who chose to keep their babies. I spoke with a volunteer and pointed out how the headlines had been intertwined forever.

But before she finished reading, her cell rang.

She answered and then barked, "You have to get out now. Mary just got a save and is bringing her here to get an ultrasound. You cannot be here!"

I grabbed my items and ran out the back door to my small Toyota, got in and zipped out of the parking lot. As I looked around the building for oncoming cars, I heard screeching and saw the grill of a huge Cadillac Escalade—just inches from my windshield. It was Mary with the pregnant girl. I pulled out, and she accelerated into the parking area.

Later, I learned the fantastic news that they saved that baby!

CHAPTER 9

I was renewed in my belief that God was not pleased with abortion. My enthusiasm returned, and I tried again. I was desperate to get someone—anyone—to participate. I decided to approach my neighbor who goes to my church. He and his kids agreed to make samples of finished art pieces with the cedar tiles. Now I had a participant and three samples to show others what could be done. I was emboldened to make a deal with my grand knight to extend my trial to our parish.

In August 2011, I cut up my remaining cedar in the garage and bought three more cedar boards. I ventured to our large family and cafeteria area after Mass with my new samples and twenty blank tiles. I began extolling the project to passersby, and the first few people smiled and walked by.

A man approached me and said, "How much do you pay for that cedar wood?"

I was taken aback. "I got about a dollar twenty-five into each square."

He said, "I throw away eight times that much cedar wood every week."

His statement made me pause. He had free wood. It would change the project immensely by removing a restrictive cost.

I was excited. We talked quickly. He was in the furniture industry, and some of his cedar boards always had holes or other defects. They would throw away a good amount.

My brain was clicking like a machine. The wood was not choice. It was thrown away because of its defects. It would add an aspect to the project I would have never considered. What an incredible idea—making art from junk material and taking what was considered junk to create art.

We talked for a bit. He was very abrupt and short in his speech. I got the impression that there was an unlimited quantity available. He gave me his card and told me to call him at work to set it up.

He suddenly stopped me and was very concerned about how I would use the wood. I had to agree that it would only be used only for the art project. I could not sell it. I agreed.

I immediately contacted my brother knights and informed them that the project had changed for the better. By eliminating the cost of the wood, we could now offer free tiles to teachers for any and all students who wanted to participate. Having that much material meant that we could expand the project from one hundred tiles from kids in our church to several thousand from all over the county!

My council officers were very familiar with the process of developing new events and new ministries. I was cautioned to go slowly since we could always expand. If I could get five or ten different schools to participate in the fall, it would be a success. We could build on the project and expand the next year.

"Start small," they said. "Let's get it started first."

I agreed.

CHAPTER 10

I set up a plan. I would make visits and present our offer to the schools. I would supply the material and pick up the finished artwork. They just had to get the kids involved. I was positive that it could happen that fall!

In my planning, I wanted to obtain a wide and diverse group of participants. I had to appeal to Protestant, Catholic, Jewish, any religion, or no religion. I was resolved to make it a human rights campaign and remove any particulars that would cause someone to decide not to be involved. I removed language, symbols, sayings, and anything else that could segregate. I removed all religious words and sayings and anything else that pointed to it as being from one denomination. I removed any wording or ideals that would cause a pro-choice person to be uncomfortable. It was fair to say that everyone wants the best for children—so I would leave it at that. I pared it down to a pure human rights topic.

Why did I need to do that? I had long noticed major problems in the fight for life: the rift between Protestant and Catholic Christians and the mistrust of Christianity by non-Christians who viewed the infighting as evidence of hypocrisy. The eruption of violence in Ireland during the last century had not completely vanished. Even in Grand Rapids, the "wearing of the green" on St. Patrick's Day was sprinkled with many who sported orange.

I have experienced many times when Catholics and Protestants resisted working together. It might be slight. It might be subtle, but the reality was that one style of Christianity refused to help the other because it might lead to them becoming more powerful. Who wanted to validate the other and then be seen as affirming their proclamations and falsehoods? One brand of Christianity might never work with another brand. They had their ministries for their people and we had ours—thank you very much. Christians were destined to fight amongst themselves to the glee of their enemies.

The abortion industry has played Catholics and Protestants like a video game because of that rift. Just like a youth who has learned a trick to get to the highest level of the latest game, the abortion industry has used Christian disdain for other denominations like a giant wall to shield their deviousness. Christian groups were more concerned about their own unique brands than working together to fight the common foe of infanticide. The abortionists have raced past these "Christlike" combatants and their dogmatic jabbing, to achieve a score of fifty three million dead babies since 1973.

I prepared my one-minute sales presentation to be nondenominational, nonreligious, and fixed with precision and accuracy on our inalienable right to life from July 1776. Surely, educators would be pleased to work with a project that aligned with United States history and human rights. It was not specific to any Christian denomination and allowed kids to make art! With the expected avalanche of wood coming, I set out to get participants, especially in the public schools.

Kaboom. I was thwarted at my hometown public high school. The teachers were nice and complimentary, and they liked the idea. However, they could not—and would not—take on a project for which they would hear complaints from legal organizations that specialized in that law.

I said that we were not specific to any church.

They asked if I might include references to God or Jesus.

I answered, "Yes, of course."

They said that was no good.

I told them that, just like in the founding of the United States, we were toning out all denominational items so that any Christian would be all right with our efforts.

They countered with questions about Jews, Muslims, and non-Christians.

I said that it was no different than studying United States history, which was very Christian. Non-Christians had always realized that Christianity was in the vast majority in the United States.

They said that, unfortunately, a lawsuit could—and probably would—be filed about it.

The result, whether we won or lost, would drain an already small budget, and the catastrophic results would include personal and immediate job losses and millions of tax dollars spent on a legal battle. They might never get to teach again anywhere else, and I would still not be allowed to be on campus.

I argued that it was not right. Outsiders were excluding me, and I represented the majority of people who paid taxes in our town. They were firm that it could not happen on school property or on school time. We could not be part of it in any way—even if we liked the idea and 80 percent of the town would overwhelmingly support this. If one person launched a discriminatory lawsuit, we all would lose. Sorry.

My failure at the public high school was the same at the public middle school. I would have to get public schools kids another way. I turned my focus to parochial high schools. I made contacts with teachers at West Catholic, South Christian, and Catholic Central. I found success at several middle schools and located a person to get homeschooled students involved. The rules for involving issues such as life were not limiting the education of children in private schools. The project was moving.

The teachers explained their needs and schedules. They were busy that fall and requested their supplies to integrate it into their plans for the fall.

"When can we receive the wood?" Now the excitement was coming the other way!

I called to my wood donor and talked to a receptionist. He was very busy, but the message would be delivered. I called again. I called a couple more times, and each time, I was assured that I would get the wood. I relayed this to the teachers, and estimated they would get it by the end of August. I believed that date would provide me lots of room for delays.

Although I worked many fifty-hour weeks that summer, I could make time to perform deliveries, pick up the art, etc. My goal was to have the art on display at our opening rally of 40 Days for Life on September 25. I would work to find a venue to display the art somewhere in Grand Rapids during ArtPrize, but I did not know where. The kids needed time to make the art, and I was cutting it close. It seemed very workable in July.

However, the days went by with no wood. August was coming to an end. Where was the wood? I decided I might have called too many times in the first week. I tried another call, and there was no answer. I become anxious and perturbed and made several more calls.

When I gathered my wits, I realized that I might have become a bother. He was doing me a favor. Why was I bothering him? *Oh no.* I thought about my conduct and how I might have blown the deal. There was nothing I could do but wait another day.

The days turned into weeks. I stopped trying to acquire new schools and focused on keeping a positive message to the ones I had already spoken to. I wiggled and weaved with their inquiries about when the wood would be delivered. I could not tell them anything that would cause them to cancel, and I assured everyone that it was just a matter of time. Maybe there were large orders, fewer employees, or vacations. My filibustering worked for a short time. Those weeks in August went by very slowly. I lost my enthusiasm. I began looking at other ways to acquire materials, but we had no budget. The free wood was an all-or-nothing situation.

By September 1, the knights were resigned to consider it a failure. All my eggs were in one basket. Facilitating the project on a large scale was predicated on having free, plentiful wood. With no wood, there was no project. I could not believe it.

I looked at the dates, and I could still get it done! What were the chances that the wood could be delivered, the kids would get their art done, and I would pick up all the finished pieces and deliver them by September 27? I was ignoring the obvious.

One youth minister in Caledonia was very anxious and wanted to be called the minute I got the wood. I was putting off the teachers and covering up the fact that I had no wood. I had no idea what had happened or what was going on. I had no answers. I was clueless.

I was called to a noon meeting on September 2, a Friday, with my grand knight. It was the Friday before Labor Day, and the first day back was September 6. With the short week, my project was cooked. He was nice and polite, but he was leaving to enjoy the Labor Day weekend. He had discussed it with the other officers, and they were all a bit embarrassed. They preferred to not make it any worse and cancel before we brought dishonor to the council. He convinced me to call the teachers, cancel, and tell them we had no wood.

There was no hope at that point. I agreed and went home. I was too downtrodden to start making the calls. It was a disaster, and I decided to make the calls on Tuesday—to put off the pain as long as possible. I was depressed.

At two o'clock, my phone rang. A man said, "Your wood is here. When can you come get it?"

"What? Yes! Of course. I will be there in half an hour."

"Do you have a truck?"

"No," I responded. My mind was racing. Everyone I knew with a truck was gone. I told the caller that I would come and get as much as I could in my little Toyota Matrix. I got directions, hung up, and tried to get help. No one was around, and I had to leave immediately. I went by myself.

When I arrived, I found a four-foot pallet with a four-foot square of stacked cedar tiles—all professionally cut—that I was being gifted from the junk stock of my donor.

CHAPTER 11

N ow my wood donor was the anxious one, and it was his turn to bother me. "Come on. Hurry up and get it loaded. We are on our way up north!" The donor was the son of one of our oldest members who I considered was on par with the saints. He diligently worked each month to make breakfast for incarcerated youths in Grand Rapids and participated in many other charitable events with our council. He showed me his garden and gave me some vegetables. He explained that his son was extremely busy, and he wanted to give us cut tiles to save us time. He could not get his staff to do the work, and he finally just cut all the wood himself.

I was so happy I could hardly speak. I started putting the tiles in my little car. With my hatchback, I would be able to take half or more of the pallet on the first trip. I asked if I could come back for the rest, which was fine.

I started stacking the tiles inside the hatchback and found more space on the floor and under the seats. When half of the 2,500 tiles were in my vehicle, I still had more room. I loaded a lot onto my front seat. It looked like I could easily get three-quarters of the pallet into my car. I kept going and piled the tiles all the way to the ceiling. To my amazement, I got the entire pallet into my little Toyota. I could not see out the back, and I was as close to the steering wheel as possible. The aroma of wet cedar was wonderful, and I took deep breaths during the trip. I had heard about cedar's health benefits, and I recommend breathing in the smell! I drove my sagging car to my church and loaded the tiles into our storage area. I called the youth minister in Caledonia, and she got the first delivery on Saturday. The project was on!

As I scrambled to fulfill the rest of the orders, I got a request from the art teacher at South Christian High School (SCHS) for two hundred tiles. I rushed them to her that day. She was grateful and told me she had an idea. I was intrigued and eager to see what she had in mind.

The wood was delivered during the first week of September, and the kids and teachers went to work. I figured that some would finish ahead of the others and I would be picking up over several days and that would allow me time to set up a display. Oh, was I wrong.

Each school had to wait until the last participant turned in his or her art piece before I picked them up. Each school needed until the very last day since there was always a student or two who waited until the last moment or forgot, and each teacher worked very hard to be inclusive and not leave anyone out. They did not want to revisit the project once I picked them up. They were doing their best to make my pickups as productive and as complete as possible. However, the reality was that I had to make all the pickups on the same day. The teacher at SCHS called asked if I could come that evening. She asked if seven or eight o'clock would work. Although it was late, it worked well for me. After the call, I wondered what she and her students had done.

When I finally arrived at SCHS to pick up her art, she was burning the ends of a small decorative rope with a lighter. She had arranged a ten-foot vertical display with twelve columns of eight tiles. It was a large mosaic, and each cedar tile was fastened to the other—one hole at the top and one at the bottom—and connected to a frame with rope. She had used her husband's drill press to put the holes in the tiles. The sweet aroma of cedar was noticeable throughout the room, along with a hint of incense, probably from her rope-burning process. It was dusk, and her classroom looked and smelled like a place of worship.

She told me how a volunteer had created a ten-by-ten PVC pipe frame to suspend the tiles. She was having difficulty bracing the frame. There were ninety-six tiles in total, and each tile was the work of one of her students in that class. I worked with her to finish it up, and it looked amazing. It was a wonderful display and message! It was so beautiful.

She said, "Do you see it?"

I was dumbfounded.

She said, "Step back."

I moved backward and looked at the background. All the tiles together were making a huge heart. She had given the students painted tiles and numbered them. They were all told to create whatever art they wanted to create on top of the tile, but they were told not cover up the background paint. When she collected and reassembled the ninety-six individual art pieces, you could see the giant heart from a hundred yards away!

Of course, in every class, there is always one student who will not get the message or get it wrong. If you look closely at this mosaic, you will see that one student positioned the background wrong, but it does nothing to take away from the overall art.

CHAPTER 12

O thers I came in contact with desired to provide art pieces. While many heard what I was doing, a female friend became upset at me when she learned I was pro-life. She immediately admonished me, almost violently, and I was taken aback by her change in demeanor. She was someone I laughed and joked with. She was fun to be around, and everyone loved her. We were great friends, but I saw a side of her I had never seen before. Her sudden anger at me left me speechless.

I approached her later, and she gave me her best pro-choice arguments. She was forceful in her discussions. She could not believe that I, as a man, could understand what a woman goes through in that situation. She could not believe I could be fooled by the pro-life message. "How could you be so judgmental and force your religious beliefs on anyone?"

When I got a chance to get a word in, I told her that in the United States we were created equal—not born free. "Everyone has the right to life in the United States, and that is what makes our nation unique. People are more important than government."

We talked for what seemed like an hour.

She listened to much of what I said, but she remained forceful— even when I told her we had DNA evidence that the child in the womb was a separate and unique human being, it did nothing to change her mind. She was so adamant and unreasonable. I was ready to walk away. Her wide, wonderful smile was gone. Her lips were quivering. Her eyes teared up. She confided in me that she had had an abortion. She told me many things about herself.

It just wasn't a good time for a child, and she loved kids. She had just been asked to be married, and she had said yes. She loved a young man and was ready to commit to him. She was not sure about her future since she was pregnant again.

She told me how she wrote to her unborn that she aborted and gave the child a name. In the letter, she apologized to the child. She buried the letter in a spot only she knows about and visits.

We hugged, cried, and agreed to remain friends. We would have to disagree on that subject. She promised that she would create an art piece for me. And she did. It was a sculpture with four red hearts attached to a single pole. The four hearts represent herself, her future husband, her unborn child and the child she aborted. The art piece sits in our church—quietly and mostly ignored—and only the artist and I know anything about the piece until now. It is a symbol of the millions of women and men who have a secret and, possibly, deep regret and sorrow from the loss of a child from abortion.

CHAPTER 13

To get more artists involved and more art pieces, I put an ad in the local paper. I called a business owner who knows librarians throughout the city. She loved the idea and let me create a display in her educational toy and gift store. She immediately connected me to a home school group, and I was promised several pieces.

I did not have containers for several hundred art pieces. I decided to make a request through my church for help acquiring shoeboxes. I had lived in town for more than twenty years, and I was aware that the world headquarters for Wolverine Worldwide was less than a mile from my church. It was a very giving community, but I did not realize what I had done until I got a call from our church to come immediately and get my boxes.

At first, I was a little dismayed that they could not wait a day or two for me to come and get twenty or fifty boxes. When I got to the church, I saw an avalanche of shoeboxes. I had never seen such a large number of shoeboxes in one place, and they were still coming in. One man told me he could get his hands on more than one thousand. How many did I need? For the next couple weeks, I was turning down similar offers and picking up hundreds more. I ended up having to dispose of hundreds of boxes.

When my collections were complete, I had picked up approximately seven hundred art pieces. It would be a nice display at the 40 Days for Life opening day ceremony. I received another fifty to one hundred pieces at our display site at GVSU. To see what the display looked like, please watch the following videos on YouTube:

https://youtu.be/o3TuH77tPHY

https://www.youtube.com/watch?v=o3TuH77tPHY&t=6s

CHAPTER 14

A lthough our opening ceremony was a time for meeting with many who shared our concern for the rights of the unborn, on the next day, the volunteers began the difficult work of public prayer at the clinic. September 28, 2011, was the first day of the 40 Days for Life fall campaign. Like any first day of any group work, those involved hoped for success. A baseball team that sends up its first batter hopes he gets a hit. A soccer team wants to exit with a victory—or at least a goal or two. On the vigil sidewalk, we prayed that our efforts would lead to the saving of a life. The vigil participants did not have to wait long. A mom changed her mind early on in the morning. It was a save on the first day!

What a wonderful way to start our campaign that year. It was especially meaningful for me because September 28 was the birthday of my first child. I could never forget how time seemed to stop that day. My wife was in labor for more than twenty hours, and we both were exhausted. After all the birthing room excitement, I ended up in a soft chair with a little package of life.

My daughter had her eyes open and was just looking around. *What is this place? What is going on? How did I get here?*

I was overcome with waves of warmth and bursts of emotion. I had been involved in microcomputers, software, programming, and customization. I had labored with software programmers and hardware engineers for months to get a machine or device to react a certain way based on an input. One reaction from one input could take months or even a year to perfect one correct response. In my hands, I held a complete human being with arms legs, eyes, and ears and complete working systems for seeing, hearing, sensing pain, eating, removing waste, moving, and breathing. And this little baby had working systems that handled multiple functions and worked together, and her brain could handle everything else. She was a living, breathing, growing human. I had so little to do with it! I realized there really was a God—a creator who could do anything and was doing *everything*.

I felt a sense of commitment to her, and the desire to protect her surged through my body. I noticed everything and anything around my baby. I was acutely aware of the nurse who was handling her. I asked her silly questions about what she was doing and how safe the building was. I noticed the air quality, any sharp edges near her, and more. My mind was noticing danger everywhere: Her blanket might be too tight. The lamp could fall over. Am I holding her properly? If anyone approached, my muscles coiled up. I was ready to do battle. I even distrusted the doctor and nurse.

I was amazed at how quickly I energized into protective mode. I have never been the same since.

CHAPTER 15

⬇

The students and teachers were told that their art would be displayed during ArtPrize. In the rush to save the project and complete the project, I did not take time to get a venue in Grand Rapids during ArtPrize. Now the task was staring at me. All of those who had been saying all along that I was not a good planner and I could not manage details or multitask were saying, "I told you so," "I knew it," and "Well, it got this far." It was late September, and ArtPrize had already started. How could I have been so neglectful? All the goodwill and all the wonderful work so far looked like a giant waste of time. How could I miss such an important a task?

I raced out to make calls. I contacted a church near the abortion clinic, but they were an official ArtPrize venue, and by contract, they could not add any other art. They set up their displays months in advance. I contacted another church, but they were pro-choice and did not want to alienate any members. I contacted a pro-life ministry, but they had no room and could not add staff to handle a daily stream of onlookers.

I talked to several more, but I was in a last-minute situation. I needed an immediate response. It was true. I had not planned well. I never thought about all the aspects of a venue, parking, or staffing. I was desperate. There was a for sale sign on a building with great display windows. I ignored that thought.

I continued to search for a better venue and decided that anyone selling a building was not going to want anyone in that building, especially if they were promoting a message that was controversial. It would be a crazy thing to do, and I did not call. I made attempts at several more places, and I was told that they were too busy to allow something like that. Some said my timing was terrible and told me to call back the next year.

I kept seeing that for sale sign in the window of that building on Fulton. I was out of alternatives and desperate. I decided to call. I practiced my pitch several times before I called. I would start to dial and then stop. My mind cautioned me against craziness. *Don't embarrass yourself by asking such a silly and obvious question. I just know that I am going to be shot down.* There was only one way to know, so I called and spoke with the man whose last name was on the sign.

He said, "I will get back with you."

As I hung up, I felt relief. I had hope! He did not say no.

I had negative thoughts. Since ArtPrize was already going, all he has to do was stall, and when ArtPrize was over, he could say he hadn't turned me down. He just couldn't decide in my time frame.

I decided to think positively and called to schedule helpers to install on Saturday. I had a crew ready and at least two vehicles. I was able to get all the tables again. I made a call to the real estate company to see if I could get a hint at an outcome. I was informed that the owner of the building was in Florida and the person I had spoken with first would get back to me. Again, we prayed and waited.

On Friday, there was no word. I called my volunteers to tell them that I did not have any news. I was greeted with disdain. What kind of show was I running? My volunteers were used to setting up pancake breakfasts or running Easter egg hunts. They dealt with certainty and hard dates and times. One volunteer was not interested in being called back at all because my project was one big uncertain mess.

I asked those who would continue if they were available Sunday or Monday. They said, "Just call. We will let you know."

They were not happy with me or they tried to console me. They said, "Well, you tried" "It was still a good effort," "Look at what you accomplished this year," and "We will do better next year."

I stared at my cell phone all day on Saturday. I checked to make sure it was charged. I made sure the sound was on. I looked to see if I had missed a call or message. I checked every half hour.

By Saturday afternoon, I had received no calls back. I called the business number I had, but everyone was gone for the weekend. I checked with my most positive volunteer, and he was okay whether we got it or not.

I checked late on Saturday night.

On Sunday morning, I checked again. By the afternoon, failure was a reality. ArtPrize was full-speed ahead, and I was prepared to deal with defeat.

CHAPTER 16

O n Monday morning, my cell rang at seven thirty.

A man said, "I got your key. Can you meet me there now?"

I stammered, "My key? What?" I was surprised at first, and then I was elated. I got my wits together and realized it was the call I had been waiting for!

He explained that the owner had no problem with us being in there.

I said, "Yes, I can come right now."

"Good," he replied. "I only have until eight forty-five. I must attend an important meeting. Don't be late."

I was ecstatic.

Just like that, the installation was on. I had to shift to production mode! I could not get volunteers, tables, and eight hundred pieces of art loaded up before the meeting. I decided to go by myself, get the key, and return home. I would get the helpers organized to do the installation later.

When the real estate agent unlocked the door, I saw the inside of the building for the first time. I only expected to have one window and an office, but he explained that I had the whole building. There were six storefront windows that were available to display the art to people walking by.

There was debris and trash strewn about. It had not been cleaned in years. I told the agent that we would be out in three weeks. We would move everything out if they needed us to or if the space was sold. He was in a hurry. After he left, I scanned the place and thanked God for this wonderful gift. Just like that, we had several windows for the display.

There was no time to lose. A couple of helpers came right away, and several more came later. We cleaned, vacuumed, and removed trash and junk. The building had not been occupied in at least three years. It had been a government office of some sort. We washed the windows, and they sparkled. It was frenzied, but many brother knights showed up. We arranged the art on tables so that every window had art.

We worked all day on Tuesday, October 4.

I returned early the next morning to do final touches and arrange the pieces for viewing. I set up a twenty-foot 40 Days for Life banner. If you were coming south on Ransom from the community college to turn left to go to the clinic, you likely would see the giant heart and the 40 Days for Life banner. The daily traffic estimate on that intersection was in the thousands on a regular day, and ArtPrize foot traffic was at least one thousand.

I was exhausted at eleven o'clock that morning, but I still had one more thing to do. A real live professional artist, who was very pro-life and who was busy displaying at ArtPrize 2011, had painted a tile for me and left it at the Omega House, which was next to the abortion clinic. Since I had a valuable parking spot, I decided to walk the few blocks up the hill. I passed the abortion clinic, and no one was praying on the sidewalk.

When I approached the Omega House, I did not see anyone. I went behind the Omega House and found the art right where the artist said it would be. It was a very well done piece, but I could not enjoy looking at it. I could sense that something was going on.

Finally I see one of the 40 Days for Life board members and she has a concerned look. I said hello, and she tried to talk to me, but her words made no sense. Something had caused her to be extremely distressed.

"Are you all right! What happened?"

CHAPTER 17

I started asking questions like a rapid-fire water sprinkler. She was not able to put a sentence together. I scanned the area, but no one else was around.

"Where is everybody?" I was alarmed.

She pointed to the Omega House. It took a while, but I was able to learn that several people were inside, including all the witnesses.

"Witnesses? To what? A crime?"

She tried to collect herself, but her words did not make sense.

I calmed myself, and we took a breath or two.

The vigil participants were discussing whatever had happened upstairs in a secluded room. They were not allowing anyone else inside. There was an air of secrecy.

I kept asking what was going on.

They were documenting what they saw and heard, and no one else was allowed into the meeting.

My curiosity was inflamed, "what happened!?"

She told me she had agreed not to tell anyone anything until they get the story approved. There had been an incident of incredible activity, and she was sworn to secrecy until the approved version of what happened was released.

My curiosity went from mild to extreme. I began to slowly pry away details from her. There was no way I could wait any longer to find out what happened.

She tried to stay silent. I sensed that she wanted to tell me, but her promise of secrecy kept blocking her thoughts. I realized the comical predicament that we were in.

Her words came jumbling out again, with many abrupt starts and stops, and her desire to scream out the story swelled up inside her. The dutiful part of her brain clamped down and turned off her voice.

In my years of call center trouble shooting and sales, I was highly experienced in obtaining information. I sniffed a challenge and quietly plotted to get the story out of her. I had a flashback to my door-to-door sales experiences. I would go to homes with signs that said: "No soliciting" or "I shoot every third salesman who rings my bell. The last two left yesterday." We knew that some people put signs up like that because they often bought from salespersons.

I came at her from a different angle. My persistence was not to violate her oath—only to gain assurance that no one was injured.

She acknowledged that no one was injured.

I replied, "No one went to a hospital, correct?"

She offered a small extra bit of information: no one went to the hospital, but there was a nurse involved.

I kept going, and after thirty or forty minutes I was able to get the whole story out of her. I later heard the official version, and this is a general retelling of what happened on October 5, 2011.

Before nine o'clock, a pregnant woman with an appointment at the clinic spoke with the sidewalk counselors. After a discussion, the woman agreed to go to get a free ultrasound with the counselors. HELP Pregnancy Crisis Aid was not open until later, so it made sense to the woman that the counselors would take her to eat somewhere and let time pass. The woman did not know—but the counselors knew very well—that there would be no ultrasound technician working that day. The counselors did not let on to the pregnant woman. They just continued on as if the ultrasound could be obtained when HELP opened. They took her to a fast-food place and bought her breakfast, but when the time came to actually go to get the free ultrasound, they were in a bad situation.

They decided to pray. To my knowledge, their prayer to God included stating to God that they had done all that they could do. God needed to do something, and they just proceeded—in a pure act of faith—to HELP Pregnancy Crisis Aid and an impending disastrous situation should someone at the clinic tell the woman that there was no technician that day.

Meanwhile, back by the vigil, a car drove into the driveway of the Omega House. Many people do this to park illegally and go shopping or attend class or visit art. Anyone in charge of the prayer vigil must approach the violator and instruct them to park elsewhere. Stopping in the driveway was a dangerous traffic concern. So whenever a car pulls into the driveway, those in charge noticed.

A woman in a medical uniform got out and called out to the counselor and prayer vigil people. She apologized for bothering everyone, but she said that she worked at the hospital and had gone to work that morning but was not on the schedule. She thought she might just stop over here and see if we needed any help. She had already put on her makeup and was dressed and ready to work. She announced that she was a certified ultrasound technician.

The first reaction by those on the sidewalk was disbelief. *Is this some kind of cruel joke? How does she know we are in desperate need of an ultrasound technician? Who is behind this seemingly evil work of the devil? Who are you? Where are you from?* They quickly realized that no one had ever met the woman. She was a stranger to all.

"Did anyone call you?"

No. She just felt the need to stop by, and that was all. Her car was still running as the stunned vigil personnel tried to make sense of it.

Our prayer vigil management members were quite awesome with details, scheduling, and tiny bits of information. Whenever I attended a planning session, there were handouts, discussions of minute details, concern over wording, and numerous other items, such as where we could and could not stand, how we were to act, and more. We could have lost our privilege to have free speech at that location if we said or did the wrong things. We could have lost our reputation as a peaceful prayer group, and people would not support us. Heaven forbid that we supply the clinic with a reason to contact the police and get someone arrested. Attention to rules and details was paramount.

How could someone have leaked the information about there not being an ultrasound technician that day? Who went out of bounds and didn't get approval to obtain this person's services? What was it going to cost? How did we not know about her?

It was an incredibly timely occurrence. When they recovered from their initial shock, they told the nurse that they needed her services right away. They rushed her to HELP Pregnancy, and she arrived to the astonishment of the staff and the counselors with the pregnant woman. She performed the ultrasound and saved that baby.

A few minutes later, a man approached with his pregnant girlfriend. He asked if the free ultrasound was still available, and the counselors were happy to report that it still was. They took him and his girlfriend to HELP. After seeing the ultrasound of his child, that baby was also saved. Another was saved within the hour.

Mary Verwys, a veteran counselor on that sidewalk for more than twenty years said she had never witnessed so many saves in one day, and in such a short time span. I videotaped Mary telling her version of this story and put it on our Facebook page (ThumbsUpGR).

CHAPTER 18

---❦---

The art was on display for three weeks, and one of the founders of 40 Days for Life, David Bereit, even stopped by for a picture.

Our campaign did experience another save in October. On the same day, a relative of the family who donated all our cedar tiles gave birth prematurely. The baby went into intensive care. She weighed less than two pounds. We prayed for several weeks, and she came out of intensive care. The doctors gave her a great health report. Although she had a rough beginning, she grew and grew. Two years later, she shows few signs of any trauma from that scary start. At the time of the prayer vigil, we saw it as a sign from heaven. The clinic typically provided a much different style of health care to a fetus at that stage in life.

Besides the additional message we received, another profound situation occurred in late October. As we arrived at the clinic, there were no vehicles in the parking lot. The clinic was closed. It was very strange because this doctor never took a vacation and was always working. He was always on time, never missed a day, and was very successful in business. One of our regrets in closing the horrible, bloodstained, roof-leaking stench pit in Muskegon and several clinics from Grand Rapids to Lansing, was that the success at closing those clinics became this doctor's prosperity. He got all the business afterward. Our triumphs had made him rich.

In late October 2011, the Fulton clinic was closed. We found out that the head nurse at the clinic was gone. She and Mary

Verwys were in a meeting at the former abortion clinic, which was now the home of Life International, a worldwide ministry promoting life and opposing abortion. I was told that their discussion was deep and personal. She had been with the abortion clinic for many years. She and Mary were almost like soldiers in World War II who celebrated Christmas together even though they were on opposing sides on the front lines.

We heard that the two leaders discussed many topics, including the clinic manager leaving the abortion business. It was reported that the head nurse had used many terms in her discussions that more truthfully describe the process that was contested, and that she tearfully admitted that, regardless of the politics and verbiage used, they were ending a life. In an honest discussion, the use of the words *reproductive health care* becomes a thin veil to disguise medical procedures that result in the death of the fetus. In our nation, founded on the rights of individuals, it is hard to argue with any conviction that our smallest humans have no rights. We heard that there were tears and hugging.

We turned to praying for a change in the heart of the clinic worker. We were ecstatic and more excited each day that there were no abortions at a place that typically did five to ten a day. I was convinced that it was finally over and that the last clinic in Grand Rapids would close soon!

Besides all the activity at the clinic during the fall 2011 campaign, ArtPrize had its own flurry of activity. Our pro-life art was on display—less than a football field away from the center of ArtPrize foot traffic. A leading contender for first prize was a stunningly huge glittering extravaganza called *MetaPhorest*. Everyone had to see it. The mural spanned almost one hundred feet in width and four stories high. It blasted its message from the side of a building. It was a message of hope and encouragement about youth. The word *visualize* was written in huge letters. It was not a suggestion. It was more of a command to not judge by what you see today—but to visualize how to improve a young person's life. The art depicted a super-sized and expressionless head of a young male with the top of the head removed. Small people were constructing the brain area. The artist calls *MetaPhorest* "a metaphorical tribute to the potential building power of the arts and Grand Rapids's youth."

It was an incredible message of life. *Metaphorest* symbolized how a human mind could be educated and transformed. It screamed out that everyone needed a positive attitude for looking at human beings. The message of the pro-life movement was to visualize the potential of what a human could become and not make a choice based on economics, timing, or anything else.

MetaPhorest was a message to adults: GO out into the world and do some small part to aid younger people! I saw *MetaPhorest* as a symbol of the Garden of Eden, but going a step further, insinuating that God has created a magnificent place for humans to be. Adults needed to go out and harvest good things, good information, and then help God with his most important creation of all: mankind. The sculpture begged everyone to refrain from making judgments based on today and to think about the future. The large head was nestled in sunflowers, which begin with tiny seeds and grow very tall. The blue skies, glitter, and color symbolized the many ingredients for success. The mind of a young person needs adult gardeners to finish development. The art depicted the need for a community of helpers to influence how a person thinks. The art hinted that our Creator expected us to be of great assistance in a person's development—and that humans should not be alone in their growth.

The message from *MetaPhorest* aligned with everything our pro-life workers were professing: Do not throw away a human being because of what you were sensing today. Visualize what could become. Trust in the Creator of the garden—and go forward instead of being negative and giving up on someone. To me, *MetaPhorest* is a pro-life sculpture! I see a divine statement in the thirty-foot face. This young man is not smiling or angry, he is blankly staring at the *abortion clinic* each day—almost as if to say, "What are you doing? Give me a chance."

That year, *MetaPhorest* ended up in second place. A much smaller work of art, a stained glass mosaic called *The Crucifixion*, won first prize. Both artists had finished in the top ten in the past, and there was negative talk about the judging of ArtPrize. *The Crucifixion* depicted how people and government allowed the killing of an innocent and blameless man, and *MetaPhorest* told everyone to visualize what youth could become.

With the Crucifixion and MetaPhorest awards, I was ready to hear more good news, but the discussions broke down and the clinic reopened. Our work was not over.

Our efforts caught the attention of higher-ups in the Knights of Columbus. They are an adamantly pro-life organization. I was asked to create a presentation that outlined our efforts and submit it for consideration for awards that were presented each year. We were awarded the Culture of Life award for the state of Michigan, and we got an international award for support of the Culture of Life from the Supreme Council of the Knights of Columbus.

Rather than quit, we continued to show the art at events after ArtPrize. After several showings, mainly at churches during events they sponsored, it became apparent that the ninety-six-tile mosaic I nicknamed the *HeartSail* was a crowd-pleaser. I nicknamed it the *HeartSail* because it caught the wind like a sail when it was displayed outdoors and because the South Christian High School nickname was the Sailors. Several viewers asked if we would display it at ArtPrize the next year. After I checked into entering it, I learned that it would not be eligible for several reasons.

After installing and uninstalling the *HeartSail*, we had another problem. The frame was not sturdy. My fellow knights and I developed several fixes, which included putting steel tubes in the PVC pipes and using cross-member support pieces. The art still would warp and be flimsy. I thought about how I could support the mosaic better.

I thought of ways to overhaul the stand. I had hundreds of blank tiles and could make another mosaic. If I had a holder that was sturdy and reusable, we could have an annual contest to create a new mosaic. We could work with kids aged fourteen to eighteen since they were ineligible for ArtPrize. The teens could submit designs, and we would vote and award the winner. The winner would be supplied with tiles and paint for a new mosaic. We could install it somewhere during ArtPrize. That would be awesome!

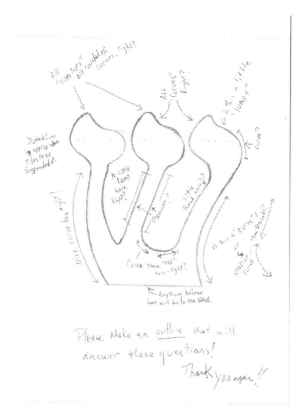

All "drippy tops" are rounded of curves, right?

All "curves" Right?

Is this a little "lumpy"

curve?

Dotted Line is approx where Tiles to be suspended.

Little lump here, Right?

Straight?

Little bend here?

Nice Curve here okay?

Curve Then "flat" here - right?

Is this a curve? or start of curve?

Start of curve or straight then sprinkle?

Anything below here will be in the BASE

Please make an <u>outline</u> that will answer these questions!

Thank you again!!

CHAPTER 19

A s 2012 progressed, I was excited to produce another event. I met with my council and told them my thoughts about a plan for our very own art contest for teens. They encouraged me—but only if I got all the details together so that it could be looked at. However, even at the idea stage, the reaction to such a large endeavor was negative. Our council could not take on such a large task. I shelved the idea.

I had another idea. In trying to make the holder for the *HeartSail*, I thought if we spent some money and made a super sturdy movable piece, that we could re-use it and change the art on the mosaic. I suggested that we enter a pro-life art piece, similar to the *HeartSail*, and try to display it near the clinic. If I could create a freestanding base that could be moved to the site, assembled, and then removed later, it would be like a pro-life billboard. I began to research and check out options.

At our Knights of Columbus anniversary dinner in March, I received our council's highest award. Later, my church gave me their first award for stewardship. Several members told me how proud they were at the state convention on Mackinac Island when they accepted the award for the ArtPeace Project. I announced that I was already planning something much bigger.

I started drawing up ideas for a sturdy base. I wanted the base to be artistic too. Since the cedar tiles represented people, maybe the base should be a symbol of our Creator. I started looking for symbols of God and found shin, the twenty-second letter of the Jewish alphabet. A large version of the shin would work wonderfully, and we could attach the mosaic somehow. I decided to get help and was told to visit a Knights of Columbus member and former art teacher. Jim Wisnewski was a sculptor at ArtPrize and taught art for many years at West Catholic and Catholic Central High Schools in Grand Rapids. He helped me immensely in my planning. We discussed materials for the shin, different looks, strength, color, and much more. Although he was a proponent of wood, I did not think wood would provide the permanence of a metal base. In an outdoor environment, wood might warp.

Jim was looking hard at the cost, but I was convinced that some sort of metal would be better. I continued my design thinking, and after several drawings, I decided to check out how to create a giant shin that we could disassemble and pack up in a semi-convenient way so that we could move the art to different locations. I found a custom steel fabricator in Jenison, and he told me that they had done several custom pieces for artists at ArtPrize. He told me he would like to do it and we met. We discussed cost, strength of the piece, how to make it movable, and how to rust-proof it. He was confident. He requested a picture to create a draft model from.

I met again with Phyllis Witte, gave her a picture of a Jewish shin, and asked her to draw an artistic version of it. I took her design to the metal fabricator, and he created a digital file that we used to create a computer model. On the computer, we created the shin in simulation, and we tested different thicknesses of metal on the computer. We tested its strength under various scenarios. We used finite element analysis and were more than 90 percent confident that the structure could withstand wind gusts of up to sixty miles per hour or a 250-pound person climbing on the structure. The shin had to be light enough to move but heavy enough to be as solid as possible.

I would need some cash to build it. I met with our grand knight and asked about funding. I needed between two thousand and five thousand dollars. The response was immediately negative—but also encouraging. We had never done anything like that before, and we were finding out how it might work as we progressed. I was asked to forget about the steel structure and just go with a cheaper option for the base. I started to think that would be the way to go.

Within a week, one of our council members called to say that we could do a special project for his company that would net us around $2,000. Maybe that money could be used for the pro-life art! I was certain that it was a sign from above to not worry so much about the cost. The wood option was not optimum. I wanted the shin to shine in the sun. Metal was far easier to work with than wood. I went ahead and decided to order production of the shin at about $3,500.

Getting a new mosaic in a short time would not allow me to put together a program to involve kids. I decided to ask Phyllis Witte to collaborate with me and enter ArtPrize with me as her art partner. She would create the mosaic, but it would be all her art with no student involvement. I would supply all the other items, the holder, the attachment pieces, installation, labor, and transportation. I would find a venue and handle everything else to get it into ArtPrize 2012. I would seek out a venue that would best position our pro-life message. Wouldn't it be great to find a location next to our last remaining clinic in town? We agreed to meet at the mall and discuss.

As I excitedly told her about this plan, she responded with legitimate concerns. She had been through much in her long teaching career. She was genuinely shocked at the amount of money I was discussing for the building of the shin. She sensed that it had a high probability of failure and told me she was not interested.

I quickly clammed up and listened. I was not expecting any resistance—and certainly not a complete rejection. She liked the idea, but she would not get caught up in the money battles, advertising, or marketing. She was very busy, and the project was a long shot at best. There was a tiny chance for success and no positives for kids, which was what got her excited to participate in the first place. It was almost selfish. She told me a horror story about a person who got into a project expecting a monetary return, was slammed with thousands in debt, and had a great project cancelled. She saw many errors, told me to save my money, and began to pack up and leave.

I was blasted with fear. If she walked away, I would have no artist. There was no time to start over with another artist. The project would die. I did not want anyone else. She created the *HeartSail*, and all continuity ended if she left. I would have to explain why she left, which would be negative. There was a presidential election, and the pro-life message needed to be out that year. I could not fail.

I immediately responded to her concerns. I reminded her that I was making good money and could put the expenses on a credit card until I got reimbursed. I raised my voice to make Phyllis comfortable. "Our council was just informed of a money-generating project for about $2,000, and I will be getting those funds. Even if I do not receive funding, I am prepared to put up all the money for this project."

She was not impressed. In fact, she went into teacher mode and instructed me not to do it without full funding up front.

I told her that the project was vitally important! I told her how wonderful she said the results were with her students. One student had no idea what the pro-life movement was all about before the ArtPeace Project was added to her classroom activities. She became a sidewalk counselor after her experience!

Phyllis agreed that her students were greatly affected, that they took ownership, and that the experience was wonderful. However, the 2012 project was clearly not benefitting students directly. There was no direct student involvement. If it did not lead to another avenue for students to be involved, she was not interested and had no time for it. She wanted no part of my financial failure and increase in debt.

Ouch! Just like that, I had lost her. I was crushed. There was a deep silence. I was silently praying for the Holy Spirit to put words in my mouth.

She was visibly uncomfortable and distressed. She continued packing up to leave.

I promised to get students involved again after the project. I promised her I would. She would have no other duties other than creating art at her leisure, and I would get my expenses covered.

She looked at me like I was lying.

I was. I had no guarantee for reimbursement. I said, "Phyllis, I was prepared to do whatever it takes—even to push to the brink of death—for this cause! Five thousand is nothing to spend to save the lives of children! You and I know that somebody has to go out of their way and bleed and suffer a bit to change minds. Who will go out of their way? Something out of the ordinary has to be done to thwart the abortionists! Even if I do not get any money back, I am prepared to accept this financial burden. I am capable of surviving. I do believe people are ready to back a project like this. If they witness it happening, they will want to support it. I just need to launch it, and it will take off."

I ran out of words. Then I blurted out, "Please do not let this project die!"

There was a pause.

She did not leave.

There was more silence.

I did not know what finally made her stop leaving, but she finally agreed. She was in, and the project would happen.

CHAPTER 20

I supplied Phyllis with plenty of tiles and she would do a similar heart design and get a mom and a baby inside a giant heart—visible from half a mile away. She would utilize the holes in the wood in a creative way. I got her two hundred blank tiles with lots of defects to start. She had a problem with drilling the holes. I found out she had a drill press with a dull bit, and we solved that issue. We learned from the *HeartSail* to put two holes in the top and bottom of each tile, not just one. The more I worked with her, the more I realized that her hesitance to do this was that she had no time to do this. It was very inconvenient and the her efforts were completely voluntary. She was awesome.

I began my tasks. I needed a better way to connect the tiles. I had to suspend the entire mosaic in front of the shin from a crosspiece of some sort. My idea for a crosspiece went through many trials with different materials. Phyllis was adamant that the crosspiece be transparent to not interfere with the viewing of the art on the tiles. I found transparent and clear plastic materials to be less than adequate for an outdoor sculpture since they break easily and drilling holes was precarious. I just didn't like transparent. I looked at iron and other metals, but the cost was high. There was a transparent material that fit her needs and allowed drilling, but the cost was too high for me. I wanted the cross to be visible. I had to fasten the crosspiece to the steel, and there would be vibrations, anything that would crack would not last. It had to be durable but not brittle—soft but not pliable. The more I checked into it, the more I wanted it to be a wooden crosspiece. I liked the biblical aspect of having the tiles hang from a wooden cross.

Jim Wisnewski and I talked about using crucifixion nails to fasten the crosspiece to the shin. I liked the idea a lot. He knew of a church off 76th street that had these nails. I visited them, and they recommended that I contact a blacksmith to make the nails. I called the oldest blacksmith in Grand Rapids, Ebling & Sons, and Jim Nammensma told me he had been to the Holy Land and made these before. He knew exactly what to do. I hired him, and he created the nails just like the Roman soldiers would have done two thousand years ago.

I provided the dimensions, and the standard nail for the feet was twelve inches so they would protrude through the back of the shin. Jim made them thick enough to fit into the holes we would drill. They were sturdy enough to hold the art, especially against the force of the wind.

I stopped by as he created a super-hot fire to forge the metal. He pounded the iron, and they cooled. He explained that the Romans made the nails for the feet much longer than the nails used in the wrists because most of the nail went into the wooden step that the person being crucified would stand on. He also explained why the soldiers were so cruel: If the unlucky fellow crucified were to somehow wriggle off the cross and make it back into Jerusalem and be sipping tea the next day with holes in his wrists and feet, the soldier who failed to secure him properly would be the next one crucified. The Romans were very concerned about Jesus. The Roman military forces in Jerusalem had been on high alert since Jesus entered Jerusalem with great fanfare. Pontius Pilate, the commander in chief for that area, gave a very public order for Jesus to be crucified. The soldiers made sure to certify that Jesus was dead. Woe to the soldier who failed to properly crucify Jesus.

The shin is a letter in the Hebrew alphabet. The first letter is *aleph*, and the second is *beit*. Those letters are where the word *alphabet* comes from. Hebrew is one of the earliest written languages, and it came about at a time when the Egyptians were using symbols that had much meaning in their written communications. The shin symbolizes Yahweh. There are books written about the shin. Many people are familiar with the mezuzah, which is attached to the doorpost of a Jewish home. The letter shin is regularly found on a mezuzah to remind that person to remember the Word of God and God everywhere a person might go. It is customary to write a scripture verse or two on paper that is inserted into the Mezuzah.

When the Hebrews drew a shin with charcoal on parchment, they would start from the same point and make three separate lines that rose upward on different paths. That showed the three different forces of Yahweh. At the top of the lines, they would make a dash to show fire. Drawing the shin symbolized that God or Yahweh was a force in motion. When something came into the path of the forces of Yahweh, Yahweh stayed the same. Whatever was in the path of Yahweh would be changed. This representation is an artistic way to show that Yahweh was bigger, greater, and more powerful than anything else anywhere.

Another description of the shin was that it was a tooth or three teeth and that the letter symbolizes cutting up or chewing. Again, anything coming in contact with Yahweh would be cut to pieces or chewed up in a positive way. Humans are remade or created into a better version after encountering God.

The three lines, or stems, represent God as Creator, Brother, and invisible guide. The Creator who makes everything—the Father of all creation—was the far left stem. The Creator was powerful, distant, and unapproachable unless we were purified. The middle stem was a symbol of Yahweh as our brother. We could become very close to Him in an impure state and relate to him like a brother. The third stem was a symbol of Yahweh as a spirit inside us and all around us. It is like the air. We do not relate to Yahweh, but Yahweh dwells within us. He is part of us.

When I first had the shin explained to me, I exclaimed that it is the same as the Trinity in Christianity! I joke when I say that the Jewish person talking to me then puts his hands to his ears and closes his eyes, shaking his head and saying, "No! He is our God, you can't have him". Besides the Christian Trinity, there are three separate forces in the deity of other major religions.

Three valleys form the shape of the shin in the promised land (the Kidron Valley). Residents like to say that God put his signature on his land. Medical persons have long noticed a shin on the human heart when viewing two-dimensional drawings of the left and right ventricles. On a map of Washington DC, a waterway forms a shin. When Spock made his famous Vulcan sign on *Star Trek*, he made a shin. If you are holding a ball in your left hand and drawing on it with your right hand, your left hand tends to form a shin, allowing you to carefully detail the ball. Did God hold the earth in his hand while affixing his signature with the rivers in Jerusalem and Washington DC?

Cedar wood is mentioned many times in the bible. Cedar wood was inlaid on altars and tall cedars were used for pillars. Eagles nested in the tall cedars. Each tile of rejected cedar had some flaw like a knot hole. Each tile is not much value by itself, but priceless to the whole mosaic. Our cedar tiles are connected like grapes on a vine. The crosspiece being the vine. If a tile is detached, all the tiles below it become detached also, symbolizing the need to stay close to the vine.

To secure the tiles with wire required something to be attached to the ends of the wire after they were inserted into the holes in the wood. I used plastic sockets from Christmas tree light bulbs. I inserted a four-inch wire in the two tiny holes in each socket used for the filament wires. I made a bend at the end of the wire and back in the other direction. When the wire was inserted from the back of the bottom hole through the front, I could pull it through. The wide plastic socket is held nicely against the back of the tile and provides shock absorption. To attach a tile below that tile, the wire was inserted into the front and out the back of the tile below, using the holes at the top of tile below, and then a socket could be inserted on the wire and the tile positioned. The wire length could be changed to provide adjustment in the aligning of the tiles. The metal shin, metal crucifixion nails and the wires on each tile offer a visualization of the flow of God's electrical energy, through the cross and the nails, to the people. The tiles are ready to be lit up with the energy from the shin—like a Christmas tree! In the bible, God calls on Christians to be lights in the darkness.

There are twelve columns of tiles like twelve apostles and twelve tribes of Israel. There are eight rows like the eight candles of a Menorah.

I wish I could say that we planned all this symbolism, but we did not. There may be even more symbolism yet to be discovered!

CHAPTER 21

I made a decision to go with a wooden crosspiece to suspend the mosaic. I decided to make the decision and not tell Phyllis. I would have to show her. She said if I couldn't use something transparent, then I should go black and as thin as possible. I could not do her bidding and get it to look like a crucifixion cross. I said a prayer, asked for divine assistance, and made the decision. I purchased a cedar board and painted it black.

Our metal fabricator needed to know where to put the holes in the shin. I thought we needed a hole in each of the three stems, but I thought about it more. *Why not have all three holes in the middle stem?*

In Christianity, Jesus is the second person. That corresponds to the brotherly aspect of the middle stem of the shin, which represents mercy. I asked about the weight-bearing capability of having three holes in the middle stem, and we did an analysis on the computer. Our ninety-six tiles and the crosspiece were well under the limits that would put any stress on the nails or the shin. I had no time to discuss it with Phyllis. I had to decide. I told our fabricator what height I needed it to be, and we positioned the mosaic on the shin via computer simulation. He got his measurements. If we did not hit the spot correctly, we could not fix the error! We measured several times. We were confident, and he set up the piece to be cut.

I took a video of him drilling holes in the middle stem, and the steel piece was on the ground while he put his knee onto the stem area. When I viewed this picture later, it resembles how

Jesus was laid on his back at Golgotha. The Roman soldiers held him down while they located the exact spots to hammer in their crucifixion nails.

Our location was important and I needed to get the art as close to the abortion clinic as possible. That year, a venue opened two doors away from the clinic! It has not been a venue since! Because the venue owner might be pro-choice, I was nervous when I called to inquire about having this art there during ArtPrize. She immediately asked me if my art was family oriented. They were concerned that I had items that kids really should not see.

I replied that I had a very family-friendly sculpture.

Later, the husband of the venue proprietor told me he was a member of the Knights of Columbus.

The venue was right where I wanted to be. I was able to select my spot. The only other exhibitor at this venue wanted to be on the sidewalk. I took the position on the busy corner of Fulton and Lafayette. At least three thousand cars passed each day, and there was great foot traffic during ArtPrize.

I needed to supply a name for our art for all marketing and the ArtPrize website. I had been watching the NFL playoffs and was amazed by the performance of Tim Tebow on January 9, 2012. I had become a Denver Broncos fan after their unbelievable crazy upset victory over the highly favored Pittsburgh Steelers, which ended in the wildest way: an eighty-yard touchdown on the first play of overtime.

This game qualifies as a miraculous win. With the John 3:16 statistics Tebow generated, 316 passing yards and 31.6 yards per pass, against the top-rated defense in the NFL that year, I was certain that God was sending a clear message to the United States. I watched the very next game as intensely as any longtime fan, rising and falling on every play and awaiting another miracle with the NFL's top Christ-honoring player. However, Denver lost 45–10. That devastating and emotionally crushing event was made worse because of the excitement created just one week earlier. I was certain that God was communicating something in this game also. He had to be providing a message! After the completely obvious miracle of the week before, I had a strong sense that I was supposed to watch the next game for a very direct and important message for the title of the art.

What meaning could come from this horrific and embarrassing loss? That you could be welcomed as the savior of the world in your capital city—only to be crucified one week later? Could that have been the message? That was what happened to Tebow in his last days as a Bronco. However, I needed a title for the art. The miracle I observed in the upset victory over the Steelers was in the 3:16 statistics. In the horrific loss to the Patriots, there were no statistics that could blot out that enthusiasm-crushing final score. Maybe that was the clue, the score 45–10. I did a computer Bible search of every verse with a chapter 45 and verse 10. After searching all, I found this most profound and very pro-life statement in Isaiah 45:10 "Woe to him who says to a father, 'What have you become the father of?' or to a mother, 'To what have you given birth?'"

Wow. In Isaiah, God was speaking directly to his people. They were in bondage and suffering greatly at the hands of their captors. Any Hebrew woman giving birth at that time was creating another slave for the enemy. Certainly those in power could view any Hebrew slave child as worthless and not of any value and mock the expectant father and mother. For myself, the verse has a direct message to the abortion industry who routinely tell anyone in a crisis pregnancy that the child being formed in the womb is just a glob of cells, worthless instead of priceless.

I called Phyllis and asked if she had ever read Isaiah 45. She reeled off Isaiah 45:9 word for word. She used that verse in her art classroom for twenty-five years! The verse had great meaning to an artist. God states, through Isaiah, that it was as ridiculous to mock anything he created as it would be for the clay to tell the potter what to make.

We agreed to call the art Isaiah 45:10.

CHAPTER 22

I set the art on an angle so it was visible to eastbound and southbound traffic. Anyone headed to the clinic from the community college could not miss the giant heart with a mom holding a baby inside the heart.

Phyllis made a beautiful mosaic and used bright acrylic colors that gleamed in the sunlight, causing many to comment that they thought it was glass instead of wood. Phyllis made half the heart gray and barren, and the other side was colorful to symbolize a Bible verse: "I set before you life and death, choose life!"

The cedar we were using was junk because of a knothole. Phyllis put pictures of adopted kids behind all the holes in the wood on the colorful side and left the holes empty on the dark side. Many years earlier, Phyllis had adopted a child with disabilities. She and her husband participated in an adoptive parents' club. Her child, now in her late teens or early twenties, was in a world all her own and would make bird noises. I learned that her special daughter loved pictures and art. With all her duties as a teacher, Phyllis and her husband took on an incredible task of caring for her. I was present when she brought her special daughter to the venue, and I got to witness her reaction when she found her picture on the sculpture. Although I missed that photo opportunity, another adopted youngster was brought to the art and found his picture while we were videotaping. You can watch that joyful happening on YouTube at
https://www.youtube.com/watch?v=d24ZbVjtXcI.

For those who are technically challenged, you can type in the address, and the Internet will find the video and load it.

Another YouTube video advertised Isaiah 45:10 in 2012: https://www.youtube.com/watch?v=iwF6uYL8stw.

We prepared the site by digging up the grass and leveling the area to install the shin. I got my brother-in-law and several knights to dig up the ground, level it, dig postholes, inset anchor bolts, and fill it with quick-setting cement. After the settings were dry, we lifted and bolted together the two hundred-pound segments of the shin. The sunlight shimmered on the silver surface, constantly reflecting rays of sunshine off the circular-brushed steel surface. We set up the mosaic on a 45-degree angle, facing eastbound Fulton and southbound Jefferson traffic. People driving to the clinic would not miss the huge heart with a mom and a baby. Our ability to withstand wind shear from our simulations proved to be the right amount. When we experienced wind gusts of fifty miles per hour, the shin did not move.

Phyllis joined our installation crew, and we wired the cedar tiles and tweaked them to be straight. The art proclaimed its message daily for three weeks. The wind, rain, and sun delivered many blows, and at the end of ArtPrize, the art needed repairs. I was present many days to explain its features to those passing by. I was there before and after my shift at the call center—more than one hundred hours.

As a registered ArtPrize sculpture and submission, pictures of Isaiah 45:10 are in the online program and part of ArtPrize history. Hundreds stopped by, but we got few votes. At the end of ArtPrize, we displayed for a couple more weeks before we removed the art with little fanfare and put it into storage.

During our display, I learned that most 40 Days for Life prayer vigil participants had no idea about the pro-life message just a few feet away. There was no save related to the art display that we knew of. I could only report that the sculpture advertised a subtle pro-life message that was viewed by thousands who drove and walked by.

A female visitor shared with me that she had chosen an abortion many years previous, but she regretted her choice. She now worked for a pro-life ministry, but she made her choice when she was young. She could not see how she could survive the pain of telling her family and friends. While telling her story, she cried. I hugged her, and she let out even more tears. She told me the tears never stop.

A young couple visiting the art had never heard about Jesus, and I told them about the Trinity using the shin and explained how Jesus died for us and said no one gets to the Father except through Jesus. The visuals of the sculpture helped make sense of several things they had heard many times before. Christians were always talking about it. Seeing a physical representation of the Trinity, and several Bible verses, made the Bible logical instead of a fairy tale. They looked at each other and asked if I could recommend a church. I told them there were many in town—of all different flavors. I recommended that they immediately begin reading the Bible and join a study group. I told them to expect to learn a lot. They were excited to start attending a church.

One aspect of the art that I did not know until I started showing it was that I could say, "You have heard it said, 'Seek and you will find,'" and they would nod. I would beckon them to move away from the front of the mosaic and view the structure from behind the mosaic. As they walked around to the back, they almost always gasped at the size of the shin. The five thousand-year-old symbol of Yahweh was made of steel. They would react as if it was invisible from the other side. I found this to be a very enjoyable method of explaining that Bible verse. Because our brains work with our eyes to focus on a subject, the brain tends to ignore background items. The tiles mostly covered the shin, you have to already know that it is there and look for it to see it behind the tiles. When visitors focused on the shin, there was a bit of astonishment at how big and beautiful the shin was—and that they had not seen it through the tiles. Many people went back in front to take another look. Their brains would focus on seeing the shin and then they would see it!

Our dealings with God are similar. It is easy to look right past this amazing deity, who created us all, who has hints all over the place, everywhere we go, yet many people say they have never seen God or any evidence that God exists. When a person views all of life as creation by God, they have a different perspective and realize how big God is—beyond human comprehension.

I told viewers how the metal shin was set in concrete. Like God, it would not move. The tiles, like people, can be blown about in the wind and could become unattached from other tiles. I pointed out how the tiles were like grapes on a vine. With the many other symbolic features, I taught Christianity 101 with each tour.

CHAPTER 23

W hen Pam Tebow was pregnant with Tim, the doctors recommended that his mom abort her son because he would be born sickly. They would have to push him around in a wheelchair for his whole life. She refused. Tim was not born sickly, and he has become a sports phenomenon. The doctors were wrong—as many doctors have been wrong for years in their predictions about babies needing to be aborted. With more than fifty million abortions in the past forty years, simple statistics and probability figures guarantee that millions of mistakes have occurred.

In the NFL wildcard playoff game on January 9, 2012, the Denver Broncos were led by Tim Tebow, a rookie quarterback with questionable passing capabilities. He did not have good statistics in Denver's recent losses. The Pittsburgh Steelers featured the NFL's top pass defense and a powerful offense. Many of their players were experienced and successful in previous playoff games. With many sportscasters and news people reporting about the NFL, statistics were very important. They were used during the weeks before and after the games on the TV and radio shows that millions of fans tuned in to. No sportscasters predicted a win for Denver. They all agreed that a struggling rookie quarterback was no match for the NFL's top defense. The task was impossible. Even Pam Tebow might have doubted.

However, they did win! The win was a miracle all by itself, but Tebow's passing statistics were mind-boggling. Within a minute or two after the craziness of the final touchdown, the focus of attention was on Tim. Millions watched as the cameras found him and he knelt down, fist to forehead thanking God for his blessings. Minutes later, an announcer stated, "Oh my gosh. He has 316 total passing yards. Didn't Tebow put a Bible verse 3:16 on his eye black in college?"

Yes, he did. Tim was famous for promoting John 3:16. His 316 total passing yards was a new NFL passing record and team playoff record for a quarterback from Denver. Tim was in the top percentage of quarterbacks of all time as one of a few who won his first playoff game. Another announcer stated that the overtime touchdown pass was his tenth pass, making his yards per completion statistic 31.6! It was another record—and another 3:16.

There is mathematical proof of a miracle. Tim entered the overtime with nine completions and 236 total passing yards. If he passed and completed for five yards on his tenth pass, he could not get the miracle. The tenth pass had to get an average yards per pass of 31.6. He could not get 316 total yards and 31.6 average unless there were only ten passes. Eleven or twelve would not work. It could only be ten (do the math).

The only viable, likely, and possible way that Tebow could finish with exactly 316 total yards passing and 31.6 average yards per pass, with nine completions for 236 yards in regulation would be for the following to happen in the overtime period in this exact sequence:

- Denver wins the coin toss and elects to receive.
- Pittsburgh kicks the ball out of the end zone or the runner is tackled on the twenty-yard line, exactly the twenty yard line.
- Denver to pass on the first play.
- Denver has to complete the pass for eighty yards and a touchdown to end the game. There can be no penalties.
- The result is exactly 80 yards are added to the 236 from regulation and exactly 1 pass completion added to 9 from regulation for 316 total passing yards and 31.6 yards per completion.

And that was exactly what happened!

Besides the two incredibly impossible 3:16 stats, the announcers found another 3:16. The TV ratings were announced, and they peaked at 31.6, the highest ratings for an NFL wildcard playoff game in twenty-four years. They asked Tim Tebow about all these 3:16's and he said that the game on January 9, 2012, was three years to the day when he first put 3:16 on his eye black. They won an NCAA championship that year, and Tim won the Heisman Trophy. Because Tim wore 3:16 on his eye black, the NFL banned the practice before he could continue his special advertising method. It was nicknamed the Tebow rule.

There was another 3:16. Pittsburgh had a third down and sixteen in the second quarter when Denver intercepted the pass. The announcer stated that the Pittsburgh quarterback threw it right to the defender.

There may be even more 3:16 items from this game yet undiscovered!

Because some would continue to argue that it was only a coincidence, God provided more to the miracle of this game. Please consider the following.

Demaryius Thomas caught the pass. Thomas is the name of the apostle who did not believe until he had his hands in Jesus's side. Thomas did not use the standard spelling of Demarius. His first name included the name of the mother of Jesus, Mary, which his mother did on purpose.

Someone I told that to had heard way too much from me and sarcastically said, "Oh, and was Demaryius Thomas born on Christmas Day also?"

I immediately went to the Internet, checked, and reported, "As a matter of fact, yes! Demaryius Thomas is a Christmas baby—born on December 25, 1987."

There were a few more stunning Tebow statistics from that amazing game.

The Steeler defense had given up only six completions of thirty yards or more that season. Tim Tebow had five completions in that game of thirty yards or more—all caught fifteen yards from scrimmage or more.

That year, the Steeler defense never allowed a pass play of more than thirty yards on third down. Tebow busted that record with a pass of more than fifty yards to Demaryius Thomas.

Tebow became the first NFL player to have four completions of thirty yards or more in one quarter of a playoff game since 1960—and of any game since 1990.

In the previous ten years, the Steelers had not given up more than two passes of fifty yards or more in any game. Tebow had three of them in one game. The Steelers had only given up one pass the entire season of over forty-five yards.

No quarterback since the NFL/AFL merger in 1970 had completed three fifty-yard-plus passes in one game, yet Tim Tebow did it in his first playoff game.

That year, the Steelers held every other quarterback under 300 yards passing, and Tebow had 316 total that day.

Tim holds the NFL record for the fewest completions to attain 300 or more yards total passing in any game.

Tebow averaged more than fifteen yards per attempted pass— one of the highest in recent NFL history for any game, and his 31.6 average yards per completed pass is an NFL postseason record.

With that last pass, Tim got the NFL record for the longest completed pass in NFL playoff overtime history and the shortest time (eleven seconds) in an overtime win.

Please see this video I made of the Tim Tebow explanation. The video is of Isaiah 45:10 on display near the abortion clinic. The music is by Third Day: https://www.youtube.com/watch?v=krXGYbWydGI.

CHAPTER 24

A fter ArtPrize, I gathered my expenses to create the art, which included five hundred dollars for a paint job, and presented to my council to get some financial relief. The meeting had a kind of hush to it when I presented my proposal. Although our council had about 150 members, many of the members are relatively inactive. The fifty or so who are active attend only a third or half of the meetings, and the ones who do attend usually only come for the food! Since the majority of our charitable projects are accomplished with less than five hundred dollars in expenses— and many of our council members are already contributing much time and money on their own—a request for a couple thousand dollars toward a project that brought in no revenue and did not specifically benefit our church—even if it provided some sort of good will in the community—was immediately subject to scrutiny. I was not prepared for the severe scrutiny.

Before I presented, a request for a couple hundred dollars was voted on and approved. That could have been a good sign. Another project was deemed worthy of a charitable donation for a few hundred dollars. A comment was made that we even had extra money in our charity budget and should use it. I was emboldened. It was my turn, and they were expecting me. I remembered how proud many of the officers were when they received the trophy the previous summer and how it was on display in our church. I asked for three thousand dollars. What happened next was one of the most devastating disappointments I have ever experienced.

I was questioned, and there were negative comments. It was a complete lambasting. I was told I did not have this or that authority and that the council did not fund businesses or make loans. I was informed that it would set a precedent and that councils were not allowed to do that. It was completely out of the realm of anything our council could contribute to. I had no foundation and no official organization to which a check could be written. Maybe I could go elsewhere to get support from some corporation. The answer was no!

Uh-oh.

I was faced with reality. I had financed the project. My enthusiasm resulted in having a mountain to climb with my credit card. Over the next few months, I made several attempts to create additional income. They all failed.

Things had been going from bad to worse at work. As with many large companies, the financial types found the fastest way to save money was by eliminating workers and cutting salaries. The pressure built. One night, I stumbled on an incoming call. I was terminated shortly thereafter.

To say my life became tense would be an understatement of great proportion.

I was faced with finding a new job. My wife and I decided to sell the house where we had lived for twenty-four years. We moved downtown to save money. That caused a great rift in my immediate family and our relatives who all lived within blocks. As my relatives and children were helping pack up to move, they found out that I was storing painted cedar tiles in the garage from my pro-life work.

I pulled into the driveway from a job search right as they were moving the art to the fire pit—with the intent of burning it without my permission. They had already started a fire.

"What are you doing?" I asked.

"We are burning these!"

I was stunned. An emotional confrontation followed as my kids, in-laws, and wife let loose on me verbally. I was aghast. They blamed my failures in the workplace on the art project. Their pent-up disgust was focused like a laser on the art they had found. It was blamed with our moving out of the neighborhood where we had raised our kids. My wife's family lived all around us. They had moved from Detroit, California, and Illinois to be near us. Our kids were losing the only home they had ever known. They got right in my face and told me that I had a mental illness that had to be fixed. They said that I needed to let go of it right then, right there, and burn those worthless art pieces that had devastated our family and taken so much of my time and money. It was humiliating and embarrassing and shocking all at once.

I was taken aback. I was speechless. I tried to stay quiet, but a short verbal exchange ensued that to this day I regret words spoken that were not interpreted correctly. I stopped them from burning the art. After much long-winded verbal scolding and several recommendations to get help, they relented and let me take my "valuables" away. They shook their heads with disdain and disgust as I removed the art and drove away to store them elsewhere.

There was good news about our move. We sold our home for a profit and found a wonderful home by the Grand River. I found a job that got me outdoors and back into sales, and I found another part-time driving job that allowed us to survive. We even remodeled our new place over the next two years.

My pro-life work was put on hold.

CHAPTER 25

A s time went on, our less costly living became manageable. The pressure went down, and I got a message from God.

I was at Mass, in the summertime. During the consecration, I hear a clear voice saying, "Build my temple." For those who are not familiar with the Catholic Mass, the consecration is a central portion of the service. We were on our knees. I felt like I was knocked backward with an electric shock. I felt that Jesus was talking to me directly and with no uncertain words. The message was clear as a bell: "Build my temple!"

I couldn't sleep anymore. I found myself doing research. I had the idea that the shin would be cool to have in an enclosed place—like how the ancient Jewish temple housed the Ark of the Covenant. I searched the Internet and found information on what it looked like and how to make the ancient Hebrew housing that was moved to the desert. I learned about the twelve tribes of Israel, the Levites, and how God gave this tribe the special duties of taking care of the Ark of the Covenant. This was the Ark from *Raiders of the Lost Ark*. Anyone who touched or looked at the Ark of the Covenant would die.

Just like in the movie, I went deep into my research. The Hebrews roamed the desert and took all their belongings with them. They set up a movable temple, and it would house the ark in a "tent of meeting" in which people could approach their "God." They were very meticulous and had specific rules, dimensions, and materials for everything they did. God could not be around unclean or sinful people—or the people would die. It was extremely serious. They endeavored to be clean, and they offered animal sacrifices to appease God for any and all sins against him.

Once a year, a Levite priest would approach God and request that the sins of the people—including those they did not even know they had committed—be absolved. They would tie a rope around this priest, and he would enter the Holy of Holies. If God was displeased at all, any mistake was made, or the priest had the slightest doubt or impure thought, God would know. The priest would lose his life. By tying a rope around the priest, they could retrieve him without having to go inside.

I had an idea. What if I worked to create an area around the shin that would be like the Holy of Holies? It would be movable, and we would put art all around the interior walls. We could develop it and make it like a Disneyland tour. Visitors could review all the items inside, and the shin would be at the end. We could put several mosaics on the walls on the inside, and involve a couple thousand student artists! We could continue Christianity 101 and add much more. It could be a wonderful experience for kids. It would be many things at the same time: a religious, educational art viewing and a fun but serious meeting with and about God. We could talk about ancient Hebrew culture, explain the shin, and put about 3,000 art pieces the size of our cedar tile on the interior walls. I envisioned a wonderful venue.

I found an inexpensive but extremely strong metal product that would allow me to set up movable walls. I got the measurements from the Bible. I found an area that I thought would be a great place for the display. I met with a design engineer who worked with the material, and we created a plan. It was going to cost around five thousand dollars. It was strong, sturdy, and safe. There were no rough edges. It would be movable, and it would be great as a public display. Was this what I was supposed to do?

After several meetings and discussions, the plans were shelved. It was too much for us.

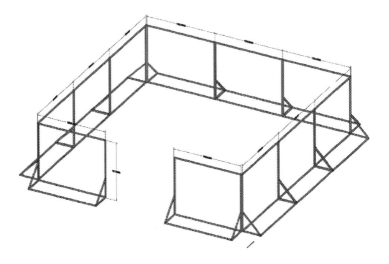

A year later, I needed to fulfill my promise to get students involved with a pro-life art project. I tried to recreate the ArtPeace Project of 2011, and I tried to build another mosaic to display on the shin.

I created a form to get students involved in the creation of the interior art pieces

THE ARTPEACE PROJECT

What is it?

It is a community-outreach program that involves youth and adults in the creation of art that is intended to give the peace of Jesus (John 14:27) to anyone in a crisis pregnancy.

Why should I participate?

There is a need to have a place to visit to see uplifting, positive messages in a beautiful, happy, joyful manner in a public venue. Youth, parents, and others who want to give these messages can create wonderful art pieces and join hundreds of others.

When?

September/October 2014 (during ArtPrize 2014)

Where?

The art will be on display at _____

Who?

The Knights of Columbus are providing manpower to set up the display.

What is involved?

Individuals. A participant signs up, either through a class, through church, with a parent, or alone.

The participant gets a seven-by-seven cedar tile about a quarter-inch thick. The participant then uses the space allotted and the medium provided to create art in any way the participant desires, using any form (paint, wood etching, pencil, nails and string, glue, foil, etc.), keeping in mind that the tile will be displayed on a wall. Sculptures will be displayed using the tile as the base and cannot be more than seven inches high.

Groups. A group could create the mosaic art for the shin holder: a nine-foot, half-ton steel sculpture. Ninety-six cedar tiles will be hung in twelve columns and eight rows with about an inch between each tile. They will be suspended from a cedar plank and attached to the shin with three crucifixion nails. Each tile has two holes in the top and bottom for wire.

Cost

Each tile costs $_____. Participants supply all paint, etc. Tiles must be at _____ by September _____ and will be picked up at there on October _____.

Where do I go to get started?

The _____ in Grand Rapids. Sign up online for more info.

Get your group involved today!

Things did not go well and the project in 2014 never happened, same as 2013. After my personal disaster of 2013, 2014 was full of job, house, and all the other issues. I did achieve one positive. I contacted the new owner (Palace of India) of the building on Fulton where our ArtPeace Project started in 2011, and asked if he would be okay if we displayed Isaiah 45:10 in that space. The office space was for rent, and they were not utilizing it. They said, "Yes. Go right ahead."

I was charged no fee. In 2014, ISAIAH 45 10 was up for the three weeks during ArtPrize. It was on display only, and there was no interaction or student involvement.

When we removed the sculpture, I talked to the owner of the Palace of India about doing it again. They said, "We'll talk next year."

They did not say no, which was a positive!

CHAPTER 26

ArtPrize 2015 was still a long way away, but I needed to come up with a plan. I brainstormed about what had gone wrong. I whittled away all the things that seemed to be important, and I focused on how to involve people, especially youth, in the art. I needed a new mosaic, a different picture. I wanted it to be pro-life and not scare anyone away. I wanted people to approach it and be comfortable. I also wanted to tell the truth about the fetus—that it was a person and not a bunch of cells like the lie told for years. I noticed a commercial that was using an ultrasound picture of a baby. It was the famous picture that went viral where the baby was holding his thumb up when the ultrasound was recorded.

What if we were to create this picture on our mosaic tiles, but we just outlined the baby and then we get thumbprints from hundreds who were walking by to finish the art? It would be made of their thumbprints. We could have thousands of people interacting with the art.

It would be so cool! Moms, teachers, and dads wandering around ArtPrize would have a destination. It would be very fun, and they could participate in ArtPrize. The Palace of India was right across from the children's museum. I just needed to get an artist to create the outline and figure out something for the background. I started making plans. The Palace of India was okay with having us! I said a prayer for guidance.

My next goal was to find an artist to create the thumbs-up ultrasound mosaic outline. I wanted the artist to be a young female, and I thought I found her when I was visiting ArtPrize in 2014. I was excited because I had met her parents, and this family was very conservative Christian. When I asked her to help out, she said, "No thank you. I am not like my parents. I am pro-choice."

If you have ever been a parent of a teenager, you understand how a set of parents with views in one direction could bring up a child who looks to another path. In the United States, youths are pressured to make up their own minds, do their own research, and not blindly accept whatever their parents tell them. Question everything! These pressures often result in them deciding to give up their belief in God and the need for going to church. High School and College aged Christians are treated with viciousness and disdain by the same types of people who call for tolerance all the time.

I would have to get another artist. I was busy with another home renovation and move. I had grown to like being downtown, but the latest house we were going to offered much and was back in our familiar surroundings. I could not refuse.

We ended up moving in 2015 after months of fixing up the Grand Rapids home and selling it. I had not worked at all to find an artist, and by summer's end, I still had no artist and no art.

I hoped that we could actually produce the project in 2015. It seemed like a winner. I mapped it out and got all the details ready so we could proceed once we found an artist. With the amount of work I was doing on the home renovation, I had no time. The search for the artist never happened.

In September, I resigned myself to letting 2015 go without a project.

CHAPTER 27

Our new house was finally livable, and I ordered cable TV and Internet. The installer arrived on Friday, September 4. We immediately hit it off since I had worked at his company. During small talk, he told me about his wife. "She is the best artist in the world."

"Your wife is into making art?" The gears in my brain engaged, and the wheels started moving. "Does she paint?"

"Oh, yes. She even runs painting classes."

This cannot be happening. The planning portion of my brain began to compute. *If she could produce an outline quickly, I could acquire volunteers to man the art, and we could make this thumbs-up ultrasound project happen during ArtPrize 2015. It was do-able!*

I had an argument with myself. *Don't call his wife. This is crazy. There is no way this can happen this year. I would have to stop everything with the house—and we do not even have floors or a kitchen! My wife would kill me first and then divorce me in my coffin.*

God can move mountains, and a little effort can lead to huge things. I was shocked by this opportunity. I had not figured out everything, but I could quickly solve the procedural steps of getting people to stop and do the thumbprint. I could get it done if I tried. *No!* I thought. *It is impossible. It is too late.* But my Knights of Columbus helpers like Frank and Mike and the Matts were used to last-minute crazy events. It could happen! Plus, if God willed it, He would find a way! Could I block God from his will? Should I block God from his will? No, this was too crazy. She is an artist. This couple was probably not even pro-life. I did not even check. All this thought process, and I bet she is pro-choice. I hesitated and then said, "I know you and I just met, but might I ask a personal question? You don't have to answer, but would you say you are pro-life or pro-choice?" Without hesitation, he said, "Oh, heavens. Yes, we are pro-life. We believe that is a baby and nothing else! And my wife is super pro-life too."

I told him about the project, and he gave me her number and told me to give her a call.

After the cable installation, I sat down to think. *This year has been great, and I have a new job. The renovation is looking good, and things have calmed down at home. I am fully involved in a home renovation, and I am doing everything our contractors do not have time for—and anything extra that needs to be done. I cannot work on any other project! There is no way. However, there is the possibility that God might be calling me. I cannot believe this.*

I looked at the calendar. If she took three weeks, I would have the art back before ArtPrize. It was just an outline, and it should not be that difficult. We had a venue—so that issue was solved. I could get volunteers to man the art and obtain the thumbprints. I would not have to be there. It could happen. I had to call her to see if she was interested. *Oh, I am such an idiot. Just because the husband said a busy wife would do something doesn't mean she can or that she will!*

I had so much going on that I forgot to call her for a couple days! Time wasted. That was probably a good thing since it was crazy to attempt it for that year. Maybe she needed six months to do anything. She would probably be too busy.

I finally made the call. She was interested. She would do a great job. We agreed to meet near her house in Cedar Springs.

I got ahold of my brother knights. I explained the plan, and they were okay with $150 to create the art. I prepared for my meeting by having the tiles in the car and a personal check for $150. I knew that the Knights of Columbus would reimburse me. I began to let the excitement come back. Maybe it could even happen that year. I left for work and was driving 50MPH down a rural road. All of a sudden, negative thoughts turned violent. One thought after another came like an unexpected summer downpour. *This is crazy. This won't work. You will stall or stop everything on the house. You will not be able to finish either project. Both will be disasters. You will get divorced. You will lose all remaining positive feelings anyone in your family has about you. The neighbors will see it all fall. You will be considered a lunatic. Selfish. Unstable. Crazy. This time, you will crash so hard you will never recover. Don't do it!*

I was suddenly incredibly emotional, and I felt enormous distrust and fear. I had visions of myself flailing and failing to make an impossible task happen that year. I saw all the contractors wondering where I was. I had committed to working on the house. I saw my wife's family members shaking their heads as they learned that I was not getting things done again. I was working on silly art things that nobody cared about. I envisioned the inevitable, painful clash with my wife. I saw my Knights of Columbus members not helping get the thumbprints. I could only see the end result of being humiliated once again. I would be an embarrassment to my children again. After all that work, I would end up nothing but a fool.

My self-doubt turned to anger. I screamed, "Why are you doing this to me, God? Why do you torment me so?" I was yelling at God! Was it some kind of cruel trick to label me an embarrassment and an idiot in front of everyone I knew?

As I was having this combination anger-and-pity party, I noticed a hawk swirling around about twenty feet above the road. I slowed to forty-five, not knowing what that hawk was doing. As I was came near it, I shouted upward, "Am I going to be completely embarrassed again?!"

When I was twenty feet from the hawk, it dove to the right of me. My eyes followed as it hit its prey. As I was passing by, it opened its wings, lifted a leg, and showed me the rodent it had snared. I looked in the rearview mirror, and the hawk was back to its normal posture.

I laughed at the unbelievable and timely occurrence. It was as if the hawk was saying, "Don't worry about anything. You have air cover." That day, I saw many hawks diving at their prey as I passed by. I laughed each time I received a message that things were in control.

"Okay, God. I got it."

CHAPTER 28

A ndrea said yes immediately. She sounded sincerely willing
to do it. I was on a very tight schedule. I had to get to my
first work-clients, finish without problems, and arrive on time
for lunch at twelve thirty at the McDonald's in Cedar Springs.
With an hour meeting, I could still get to Traverse City in plenty
of time to pick up a package at UPS, which was only open from
4:30 to 5:30.

We ate, and she sounded perfectly capable for the job. As
I was leaving and ready to give her the check and the wood, I
remembered that I had something else to give her. I put my keys
and briefcase on the front seat and opened the back door. I quickly
hit the open locks button to make sure I did not do anything
stupid like locking my keys in the car, but I bumped the button
as I slammed the front door shut, reversing the button, and locked
my car with the keys inside.

It happened so fast.

I panicked. I asked if she could take me to my house to get
my spare key. We would be back in about forty-five minutes.
She was okay with that. I could not find the spare key, and then
I remembered it was in the car. As we traveled back, I called
the police. They agree to jimmy the car open. Embarrassed but
extremely relieved, I gave her the wood and check and made it to
Traverse City on time.

Andrea finished the art in less than a week! When I picked it
up, she had created a wonderful nebulous background space with
several clouds that looked like babies! They were subtle and hard

to find, and it was a great surprise. I was able to talk a bit more, and she told me she was very pro-life. She believed no mother had the ultimate say over the life, liberty or anything that determined the happiness of a child. In fact, she did not know who her father was until just a couple years prior to our meeting. Her mother had a mental illness. She bore Andrea, but she refused to specify who the father was on the birth certificate. She was prepared to hold onto that secret forever, but Andrea was able to get it out of her after 30 some years of trying. She found her father in Chicago in 2013. He was also an artist! They look alike and have many similar characteristics. It is a wonderful story.

I obtained the same room to display our art at the Palace of India. We were allowed to display at no charge. I frantically called on my knights, and they were very helpful in getting all the tiles drilled. We assembled it at the Palace of India and put it up in the display area. However, I failed to get any volunteers to take thumbprints. I was out of time. For 2015, we just displayed the art, which was an outline of the ultrasound baby with its thumb up.

We had no involvement with passersby, and, in a sense, failed.

CHAPTER 29

---✦---

The good news about the failure to get volunteers in 2015 was that I had plenty of time to get ready for ArtPrize 2016. Since 2016 was an election year, it was better to work out all our issues and do a great job.

I found tepid interest, at best, in my Knights of Columbus council for a year long project culminating at ArtPrize 2016. There was nothing I could do about my reputation at this time. I was considered goofy, off the wall, and crazy.

Although the display of the art at ArtPrize 2015 achieved no thumbprints, I had for the first time—after five years of gargantuan efforts on my part—a complete, ready-to-roll project for 2016. I had all the pieces of art, the huge steel shin holder, the crucifixion nails, and the crosspiece. I found the artist, and she created a beautiful work of art with paint that could withstand outdoor elements. I could display it 24/7, and we could set up the art anywhere. The art was ready to be painted by the public and be personally interacted with by hundreds—maybe thousands— at any event I could acquire a display venue. I had even already established a venue at ArtPrize, at no cost, right across the street from the Children's museum. We were right on Fulton and anyone going to the abortion clinic from GRCC, the nearest customer source for that clinic, would not be able to miss our art. In an election year, the issue of life was a major point of national interest.

Could there be any other subject our council would consider more important in 2016? Oh yes, plenty. We had a pancake breakfast and needed volunteers. We needed to resurrect some members who we had not heard from lately. We needed to get volunteers to make and sell Christmas pies, and we had our cool custom apple sales coming up. I sat in the meeting and just stared. *Should I bring up the ArtPeace Project at this time? Should I risk those groans, the negative reactions, and the snickering remarks?* I had no idea how anyone would react to hearing about a project that would take half of 2016 to complete and involve at least two thousand volunteer hours. I needed fifty members to work about ten hours each to complete the project. I chose to sit and listen.

One of our oldest members, a stalwart volunteer of thousands of hours, had worked many events and was such a blessing to so many. He was a military veteran and was in pain and had difficulty walking. He had been dethroned from his longtime position running pancake breakfasts due to the need to make changes, and he was announcing his last project for our council. He announced that he had completed research on a new program to introduce to our council and needed our support.

The meeting went quiet, and all ears perked up. He had the volunteers ready to make a huge project happen. My mind was racing. I remembered him talking to me about it, but I was a little fuzzy. I had told him I would support him. We all listened, and you could have heard a pin drop.

He wanted to start up a young man's version of Knights of Columbus and run it like the Boy Scouts. Because the Boy Scouts had adopted new rules that were contrary to the beliefs of many Christians—similar to what happened in the Girl Scouts—the program could be very popular in our area. It definitely aligned with much of the work I was doing. It definitely could be huge.

He had been involved with the Boy Scouts for many years. He had connections all over the state. Our council could lead the way to get it going, and then our council could be the one all other councils looked to as they installed the program. The project could grow to epic proportions. The Knights of Columbus needed our very active and efficient council to lead the effort! The youth of America was at stake.

The members wriggled in their seats. *How could anyone not want to do this?* Our American heritage was being attacked—and even the Boy Scouts had caved to the pressure to discontinue its Christian heritage.

My heart was racing. What had I told him I would do? I started to remember. Oh no!

He said, "And to get this project going, I already have a chairman who will handle all the details and all the paperwork and work with the kids. He knows computers and already committed to helping." I slid down in my chair. "And the chairman will be… Patrick Keeley!"

CHAPTER 30

I wish I could say that I was thrilled with the honor. I should have been. I knew I should not accept the chair position, but I could not turn it down. God must have had some sort of plan in mind. I could not imagine what it was. I did not know. I decided to go with the flow and agree to be chair.

Rather than bringing up the ArtPeace Project at that time, I announced nothing at the meeting. Later, I tried to let several key members know of my plans for the art in 2016 to avoid surprising them when I kicked in and accelerated. If I got the youth project rolling, maybe the youths could volunteer at ArtPrize to help get thumbprints on the art! I prayed and moved forward.

In January, I had several meetings about the new youth program that were highly ineffective and I uncovered several issues that I considered roadblocks to doing the project. Although the youth program was honorable and good, the required paperwork of the Knights of Columbus was a huge mountain that was removing any progress we might make. The biggest delay was the liability of our council with men working with youth. The troubling remnants of the worst nightmare of Catholicism at the turn of the century: Catholic priests molested young boys, and higher-ups covered up the crimes. It was like a flood, pushing us to the side and drowning us in rules.

After several more meetings and much paperwork, I saw that the efforts required to launch this program were not worth the benefits. I knew the intentions of our council members were pure, but I canceled the project in no uncertain terms. With great knowledge of the disappointment that it was causing to one of our longest members, I could not be nice or considerate of the hurt feelings.

I completely smashed it by resigning. Continuing to flail would have caused more harm than good.

CHAPTER 31

I went full-speed ahead on ThumbsUpGR in February 2016. With my promise to Phyllis Witte to get youth involved, I went to the three Christian high schools and proposed a plan to have the kids help me get several hundred thumbprints by sponsoring an event where I could arrange to have the art on display at their schools.

I thought I could train the students to get thumbprints and words of encouragement from parents, students, and others. Maybe they could do it along with another event or fund-raiser. I could even make it into a contest, and the schools all played each other in sports. There could be rivalry. It sounded simple, and starting in January, I would have plenty of time. All they had to do was schedule an event.

In April, I made the decision to stop the effort. It was a complete and total failure. I believe it was too new, or required to much from the schools. There were too many happenings on their calendars. The school competition idea was a waste of many hours, and we had no events. It was April, and I had not one thumbprint.

Oops. My artist did attach the first thumbprint. I had one. Oh, brother.

I started to hear mocking and disparaging voices.

I was desperate for an event. I heard about a Grand Rapids Right to Life fund-raiser called Bike and Hike. I had contacts there and made a call. I had attempted to work with RTL in the past, and the efforts had mostly failed. They knew who I was. I had a reputation, and it was not good.

I was greeted with the same responses as before. However, after five years, I finally had complete answers to the standard tough questions.

Yes, the art was ready to thumbprint. Yes, I had all the supplies for the kids to put their thumbprints on the cedar tiles. Yes, I would clean the participants up and have water and wipes to keep acrylic paint off their clothes. Yes, the art weighs more than half a ton, but we have installed it many times. It rests solidly on the ground and does not tip. Yes, I would be there the entire time. No, it costs nothing. No, we are not fund-raising. No, I don't need volunteers to set anything up. We will provide everything. I just need a spot to display. No, we are not pushing any religious theology over another. It is a pure human rights effort that appeals to anyone and anybody of any faith and any nationality. Yes, it should align perfectly with the goals and themes of Right to Life. No, it competes in no way with any other youth effort that RTL is working on. We want to supplement your efforts. No, we are not handing out any literature or trying to push anyone's agenda. It is completely paid for. We will clean up, need no electricity, or will not destroy any property. Our council has insurance.

We got our first venue! The kids and parents all had fun, and I got wonderful testimonies. The minor problem was that my knights loaded me up and set up at the site. I had to grab volunteers to help me get the art packed into my van. But I found volunteers, and it all worked out. [thank you Mike and Dr. Brennan]

I was on a roll. I had two more events in May at my church in Rockford: a movie night and a yard sale. One of our members' wives was an actress in the movie we were showing, and we advertised the event locally. Our yard sale was at an outdoors venue, and I got thumbprints and great testimonies, including one from our seasoned knight who I had spurned with the youth program. He and his wife had adopted many years ago, and she was adopting. He would be getting a grandchild!

We got another venue at the Pregnancy Resource Center on Cherry Street. I heard about the venue through the Knights of Columbus. I called and got through to the event planners, and we made plans to meet.

On the day of the meeting, I stopped to get gas. As I got out of the car, my cell rang. A distressed customer needed immediate support. As I calmed the client, I realized I needed to multitask. I got out my wallet while I listened to the client's issue. I swiped my credit card and held my wallet in my left hand. I offered some solutions to my worried customer while the gas was pumping. I looked into the car and saw the wrapper from my last burger. I grabbed the trash to dispose of it, and the customer brought up another issue. I had no immediate solutions but I kept brainstorming the problem as I threw away the trash and put my wallet in the car and sped away.

I arrived at the PRC on time. It is right next door to Planned Parenthood. They are daily combatants. One wants to make a buck on an abortion, and the other is trying to save a life. They have similar online ads, and it is common for one to get a client who wanted to go to the other one! Whenever a person who is leaning toward having an abortion calls PRC inadvertently, they are in a life-and-death situation and do their best in the few seconds they have to turn the client or get that person to come to their place first: "Just check out your options." What they do daily is nothing short of heroic.

I met with management and explained ThumbsUPGR. It was a go. I checked out the site, and they had a stump on the spot I needed to use. I could have that spot, but they could not pay to have the stump removed. I told them stump removal was on me. It was not that big, and I had removed many stumps that size. They were very happy since it would save them money. After the event, they would be able to do the landscaping they wanted to do! It was a win-win situation! Hooray.

I went back to my car to go to my next appointment. I realized my wallet was not in my pocket. I had put it on the floor of my car when I was at the gas station. I opened the door and saw the wrappers on the floor instead. I could not find my wallet. *Oh no!* I rushed back to the gas station, but no one had found a wallet. I looked in the trash, but it had been emptied. They were okay with me checking, and I went to the big trash bin to grab a bag or two. I found no wallet.

For those who have ever tossed their wallets in the trash, we could start an organization or a help group for other people who have tossed their credit cards, drivers' licenses, library cards, rewards cards, gift cards, business cards, and receipts into the garbage. We could set up a place to visit or someone to call so that they can scream at the top of their lungs in anguish or just listen to someone else who has done something just as stupid. In time, they will be laughing about it instead of considering breaking things and pulling out their hair!

I contacted the credit card companies, got a temporary license, and bought a new wallet.

CHAPTER 32

I arrived back at the PRC and removed the stump after a two-hour battle with roots. On the day of the event, I arrived with two knights who were on their first campaign with me. Hap was a stalwart veteran of hundreds of Knights of Columbus events. Besides his many charity works, he had made the coffee for almost everything that ever happened at our church. I hope to be as active as he in my eighties. However, he was unable to help with the lifting of the two hundred-pound pieces of the shin. He was perfect for holding the door of my van open.

Steve and I assembled the shin and put up the art. I trained them on our first high-volume event. We mapped out the processes. At the RTL Bike and Hike, I learned that it was better to have one person do the camera and clean up, one person put a drop of paint on thumbs and show each person how to print it on the art, and one person get people's testimonies.

As the people were coming, we were operating like clockwork. We were a well-oiled machine. It was very hot and sunny, and Hap worked like a trooper but informed us he had to get something to eat and left for a bit. It was a then two man process and we still got incredible testimonies and many thumbprints. The event was a great success.

When I got home, I worked to get another event. It was summer, and I really wanted to train more of my Knights of Columbus members. If we were slammed now, I could imagine what it would be like at ArtPrize. The volume of people was many times more. Would we get jammed up taking thumbprints? I heard about a festival that a church in Wyoming, MI was doing, and they were looking for vendors to display. I tried to find out who, but they did not know. It was a Catholic church, and it was Hispanic. *How many Catholic churches for Hispanics could there be in Wyoming?* I found one right away and called. The woman who answered the phone did not speak English. I hung up and called again a few hours later. I found out that it was not their church. It was Saint Joseph the Worker Parish. I got through and set up a meeting. I went to the park to meet with their event team and found a perfect spot. I needed to have the sun hitting the art so that the pictures were illuminated.

On the day of install, I was completely forsaken by my knights. I had no helpers on a wonderful weekend in July. I took my van to our storage and started to think. If I could get loaded up, I could ask for help to teardown—just like at the Bike and Hike.

My manpower issue might be ending the event before it started. I could get the three stems of the shin into the van on my own—I had lifted them in the past all by myself—and I could get a grip on them, even though they each weighed about two hundred pounds. The base was closer to three hundred pounds, and it had no thin area to wrap my arms around. I had to think. I had to get going.

I said a prayer and backed my van to the shed. There is a ramp going up to the door, so my van is angled downhill about twenty-five degrees. If I could get the big piece started into my van, it would be going downhill as it was being pushed in. *How can I get this piece up and over the edge of my van so I can push it in?*

I went into Egyptian stone-moving mode. The base steel piece was stored on wooden boards. I realized that I could steer the base and slide it on the wood. I began to move it toward the door and noticed that I had to go over a doorstop. I put down a board and pushed it forward. It raised the front up. I found more wood to make the base go higher and realized that I could push the base on top of the wood and over the edge of the back of my van. If I continued, it would be completely in the van. It worked! I was sweating, but the worst was over. I got the other three stems and all the other art inside and headed to the event by myself.

CHAPTER 33

W hen I arrived, I went to find helpers. Two nicely dressed Hispanic men were waiting at a table for the festivities to begin. I approached them and told them I needed a hand setting up a large display. I had ten dollars each for them if they could spare thirty minutes. I told them they would get sweaty, but I was desperate. Their answer was classic! They did not say no, and they did not say yes. They said, "Do you have power tools?"

I have seen many reactions to my crazy ideas and needs from many people. What a wonderful and beautiful reaction to a person in need of help. It was exactly what I needed to hear. It was a way of saying, "Yes, but under a condition. I will help you if you have thought out your request for help and have thought about your helpers so that the helpers can count on you. Have you done your homework and prepared for getting help? Will you waste my time? If you were trying to cut down a tree with a handsaw, I might be too busy sitting here and waiting for the festival to begin!"

I said, "Yes! I have power tools!"

The two wonderful gentlemen proceeded to save my butt. We got all sweaty as we unloaded the shin and positioned the two hundred pound pieces for assembly. They used our ratchet to fasten all the bolts and my drill for the screws into the cover plates. I had plenty of wipes to get the grease off their hands, and they cleaned up. We were done in less than thirty minutes. They were such great help, and then they refused to take any money. I never got their names.

The festival was awesome, and I got the Wyoming Fire Department's thumbprints and many awesome statements, including many in Spanish! Our grand knight took time out from his farming to come down to help on Sunday. When the weather worsened, we decided to load up and leave early. Two people are needed to disassemble the art, and together we deinstalled it and put it back in storage. I found out later that we disappointed many of the festival workers who wanted to thumbprint and hoped we would be around after the festival so they could add their thumbprints.

After the event, I felt confident that we had all the main issues with obtaining thumbprints in a high-volume scenario. I knew what we had to do. We would be tested mightily at ArtPrize.

I was able to take individual tiles to a couple more places to get thumbprints, but I spent the rest of the summer planning for the big event. However, summer was not a good time to get commitments for a September project. I went to the last day without enough volunteers to do the work.

Thanks to the long lead time, I had an installation crew to get the art up. I ran aground on the volunteer issue, I had too many open hours to fill! I wanted to man the art with three people at a time. I did not know if it was because we were not collecting money, or if it was costly to get to the site, or if it was an issue of parking. It was like pulling teeth. I only got several days covered. Because of my job, I was able to get to the site at night and for a few hours during the day almost every day of ArtPrize. I resolved to get as many thumbprints as I could by myself.

The next section contains comments and encouraging words from many of the thousands of people who stopped by our art.

PART 2

TESTIMONIES

—————❧—————

If you are experiencing difficulty caused by uncertainty from an unplanned pregnancy, this section is for you!

An unplanned pregnancy is a life-changing event. You will never be the same. Maybe you do not know anyone who has been through raising a child in a crisis pregnancy situation or you do not have any type of support. Maybe you feel incredibly alone—and everyone is telling you that abortion is the only solution.

Please read these wonderful words of encouragement and wisdom that follow. Many have been where you are!

Please also take time to visit our face-book page, ThumbsUpGR, to see many more pictures of people wanting to give you a thumbs-up in your time of scariness. You can see hundreds of their smiling faces!

ThumbsUpGR is a multimedia project designed to involve many people in the creation of art and to post words of wisdom via our Facebook page to those who are in crisis pregnancy situations.

In proclaiming the message of life, one must consider a time period—and not a moment in a lifetime. Whoever looks at an acorn and states that it is just a little bit of nothing is somewhat foolish. The ArtPeace Project had an acorn start, but we invite you to see the huge sculpture we have built over the years for people to visit! Our most recent campaign, ThumbsUpGR, needed the help of the community to finish the painting—one thumbprint at a time. More than 2,500 people contributed!

We used components of great religious meaning in the sculpture.

Our ninety-six-tile mosaic was composed of rectangular cedar tiles that were deemed junk by the furniture industry. Grand Rapids is the office furniture capital of the world, and cedar wood with knotholes is usually burned or tossed away. The wood deemed worthless is our main ingredient. Many visitors do not even notice the holes in the wood until the defects are pointed out! Once the defective wood is painted or given a purpose in the art, the defects become part of the look. The individual pieces became priceless components. That was the message we wanted to convey to pregnant moms who were debating the worth of their offspring!

All the tiles are connected like grapes on a vine. If one tile is disconnected, all the tiles below it come off also. The message is that all are important!

Why did we do this? My goal was to present a very troubling, very personal, and very controversial subject in a different and amicable way. In my opinion, the major media, politicians, and health care industry have softened the words that describe the "process" of making a woman "not pregnant."

The TV and newspapers never consider how many pro-life people are aghast at the techniques to remove fetuses. Many pro-choice advocates have never seen what really happens—or they were in a mind-set and refused to acknowledge the obvious truth.

We used a painting of a digital picture from a state-of-the-art medical test, which spawned a cool new thing to do: publish your ultrasound picture on social media.

Although we were mild-mannered, friendly, non-confrontational, and peaceful, we exposed a naked truth.

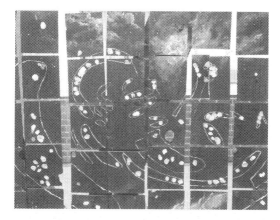

This is a baby.

Testimonies

Our goal was to get three thousand thumbprints to finish our art. The main image on our ten-foot-by-nine-foot mosaic had to be be visible from half a mile away. It was our artist's version of a famous digital picture first viewed on social media in 2012, which scored millions of reposts in the first days after the initial post to friends of the parents! I called this picture *Thumbs-Up Ultrasound*. If there were such a thing as VARF, viral awareness ratio factors, this image would be one million to one. One million people were estimated to be aware of the image versus one who had never seen it. It was so popular that almost everyone in the United States is familiar with the ultrasound picture of a baby in the womb holding its thumb up.

Besides involving the community in a pro-life activity of painting the art sculpture, we sought advice from participants, especially those who had been in that tough position. We asked them to share words of encouragement so that we could present their stories or wisdom to women who were experiencing difficulty in a crisis pregnancy situation.

In the beginning of the project, I met a woman at a supermarket I was working at. She was excited to tell me about her ministry at her church. I listened intently to her enthusiasm, and she asked if I had a ministry.

I told her I was working to acquire thumbprints on a large art piece to spread the positive message of life. She immediately became very excited and demanded to be included in the project! Since I had the paint and several tiles in my car, I made arrangements to meet her during my lunch hour.

She told me about her fourth pregnancy. Burdened with three children by more than one father, and having no father at home, she was facing what was considered an almost impossible situation: a single minority woman already working two jobs with a fourth child on the way and no father to help.

That was in the 1980s, and abortion had been around for about ten years. It was still a new and radical idea at the time.

This is her story in her own words:

> Thirty-four years ago I was in an abortion clinic. They showed me what they were going to do, and after the demonstration ... I couldn't do it. Today, my thirty-four-year-old daughter who I was gonna abort is the most loving, compassionate... (crying) I could not have asked for more. She hugs and kisses me every time we meet, and she calls me every day to see if I need anything. Of all the kids I chose, she truly cares the most about me. She is a godsend.

Later, she posted the following story with a picture of her with her daughter (see the ThumbsUpGR Facebook page):

> Oh, I give God glory for all the barriers that were put in my way to prevent me for making the worst decision of my life. I know it can be overwhelming when you have an unexpected pregnancy, but stick it out and don't end your baby's life. Abortion is not the answer. There are other solutions. By the way, I had a great support team in helping me raise all four of my children. I went far to adopt a young man who is now twenty years old. Kids are drawn to me now. If I can help any struggling parent, I reach out because I was one of them. I will never forget where I came from. My daughter's birthday is Saturday. She is my sunshine and my everything. She changed my life!

She told me that she even bought her daughter a house!

Abortion was a bad idea for her. The doctor and staff did not consider that this woman carried into their abortion clinic a person who would bless that woman for the rest of her life. They were ready, willing, and armed with deadly medical weaponry to dismember and extract from this woman, her child, her lifelong blessing, who would turn out to be the most important person in her life—not to mention a great person for everyone else to meet!

People who have lived for many years still remember the time in the United States when abortion was considered as horrible as the plague. It was an unthinkable. It was a serious option. Many people could not understand how anyone would ever consider such a severe solution to a problem. But whenever a new way of thinking or new dance or new fashion comes around, people are always open to trying out the new way. That was the case in this situation. Her motives were likely influenced by the talk at that time, and she listened.

Maybe things would have been better off if I didn't have so many children. My life could be much better. I could better deal with the situation I already have and have more control of my life. Maybe I would be freer, and my finances would be better. She listened—as many women listened in the 1980s. *Why not try this new medical procedure called abortion?*

Today, we look back on more than forty years of abortion. We can see the extreme use of abortion. In China, female fetuses are almost automatically aborted. Future women are extracted from the womb and destroyed by the government. Today, there are more than twenty-five million more men than women in China! That unnatural occurrence is blamed squarely on abortion. Many talk about government meddling in a woman's reproductive rights. Even those who are okay with abortion are alarmed at the result of government enforcement of abortion and family planning.

A coworker at a call center overheard that I was creating a pro-life art event and loudly stated that she had a story to share about a horrible experience with abortion.

A male coworker yelled, "Are you talking about your son?"

The woman replied affirmatively. Apparently, the other coworker knew of her son but had no idea that he had been the subject of an abortion discussion at the time preceding his birth.

I asked if I could interview both of them. They said yes. I had no idea how much I would learn!

If you would like to see the interview, I posted a video on our Facebook page (ThumbsUpGR) with a black-and-white picture of D-Day in June 1944.

The woman and her father suffered ailments that caused them to be less active and restricted their athleticism. When she got pregnant at twenty-nine, she knew that her checkups would involve warnings. In the 1990s, Ob-Gyn departments endured severe anxiety after several lawsuits resulted in multimillion-dollar awards over childbirth issues. The doctor at the hospital went beyond a warning in that situation and predicted that the child would be born with severe disabilities. The doctor recommended that the child be aborted.

My coworker was not interested in possible problems. It was "her baby," and she did not believe in abortion. Her doctors were sarcastic, and the nurses were going through the motions. The exciting atmosphere many expectant mothers were provided was not provided to her. On the day of the birth, her pent-up anxiety exploded in a tidal wave of disappointment when her little funny-looking package came out with one ear folded over. Even her husband gave evidence of the trauma he was experiencing over the months. He let out a groan upon seeing what appeared to be a defect. The nurse casually flicked the ear back up. The baby was fine! The medical prediction and doctor's advice were the only things that needed to be aborted!

The story did not end here. It turned out to be the only child she had. In my interview, I learned that the child would grow up to be described by his pastor and my coworker as the best youth minister on the planet. His friendliness, genuine concern for others, and ability to take charge of a group of people and provide for their needs was inherent. His pastor described an event that was typical of this young man: He took off work, thus losing income, to be a counselor at summer camp. Each night, without anyone prompting him to do so, he made the rounds and checked that all the kids had their meds, prescriptions, and personal items taken care of. When I asked the mom if this was something he was taught, she told me about her father. He landed at Normandy on June 6, 1944. He was a medic in the army. Although carrying no weapon, he raced about to supply medical aid to American and German soldiers!

If that child had been aborted, as incorrectly prescribed, she would have had no children. The line of family members with that inherent caring for others might have been stopped. Today, there is a swim program in Grand Rapids where more than nine hundred inner-city kids have learned to swim because of the grandson of a WWII hero!

I met two young men who worked with youth and adults to convert them from their addictions, mainly drugs and alcohol. They agreed that our society has many ailments—and that abortion was not good medicine. They said, "Jesus is for anything that produces life. Choose life. Jesus Christ is known as a living... as the living God who will provide all you need."

Before we set up at ArtPrize, where we received the vast majority of our thumbprints, we had several smaller events. One of the events was a men's conference at West Catholic High School in March. The men I spoke to that day were on a break from listening to speakers. Here were many of their quotes and stories.

KEPHA Men's Conference at West Catholic High School

- "Celebrate life—raise a saint."
- "Blessings come when we least expect them."
- "Choose life."
- "Life is good."
- "You can do it!"
- "Life is always precious."
- "Jesus said, 'Be not afraid. I went before you always. I know your journey has not been easy, but know that Jesus is with you always.'"
- "God loves you and your baby. Save a life. Seek God's will."
- A sidewalk counselor and teacher: "There are options. There are people who want to help. God bless you!"
- "Life is love."
- "Life is great."
- "Life is irreplaceable."

I recognized a conference attendee from my Bible study. He was a medical practitioner who had recently experienced the loss of a daughter in her early twenties in a tragic car accident. I had heard his personal testimony in our Bible study over the past year or so, and I had shed tears with him! I had seen him go from depressed and angry to obliging the will of God in his life. He prayed every day, and he constantly received perfectly timed messages in our Bible study.

When we read a chapter in our study, we normally took a verse and went around until the chapter was completed. He told us that, unbeknownst to us, the verses he read were perfectly meaningful to him—and incredibly timely! Since he started attending our Bible study, he received several direct messages that only he would have known would be applicable to his current issue. He became a joyful blessing to everyone he came in contact with, and he often found himself sitting beside someone on a plane or with a patient who had also experienced a death or a great personal tragedy. His ability to counsel those people has proven to be great medicine!

It was such a joy to see him smiling, thumb-printing our art, and attending the conference with his father. He said, "No matter what challenges you have, with the help of Jesus, you are *equipped* to handle them!"

There were more:

- "Your child is beautiful in the eyes of God. Be open to prayer. Your soul can communicate with God."
- "Know that God's love is unconditional. Choose life. Whatever seems impossible today is manifestly possible in Christ!"
- "I wouldn't have my sister if her mom had chosen to abort. Her birth mom was severely injured in a car accident and bedridden while pregnant. She gave up my sister to adoption."
- "What would I say to a person questioning whether to have an abortion or not? No!"
- An Air Force jet fighter pilot: "God bless you!"
- "Choose life."
- "Life is wonderful."
- "Choose life."
- "Choose life—trust your heart."
- "Everybody is worth it!"
- "I know a girl who had an abortion, and at this point, she seeks forgiveness and speaks out against abortion. I recommend you choose life!"
- "My daughter was diagnosed with possible spina bifida. We had her, and she is perfectly healthy! I can't imagine my world without her—spinal bifida or healthy!"
- "None of us planned on my oldest granddaughter, but God did—and I couldn't have become what God wanted me to be without her."

Men's Bible Study at Berkshire Hathaway, Michigan Beltline (Three Mile Office)

- "I am a graduate of Notre Dame, an ordained priest, and live in Oregon. Choose life!"
- "I am for life."
- "Choose life!"

HELP Pregnancy Crisis Aid

- "Have that baby, we love that baby!"

Bike and Hike—Grand Rapids Right to Life

- From a dad: "Life is more than meat, and the body is more than raiment" (Luke 12:23).
- "In Him was life, and the life was the light of men" (John 1:4).
- "Everybody deserves a chance at life."
- "We're expecting two great grandkids—can hardly wait!"
- "Life is great—so choose life! Look to God for help."
- "Life—what a beautiful choice!"
- A mom: "I have a cousin who became pregnant. The doctor told her if she had this baby, she would die—baby also. She could not abort her baby though. She got a second opinion. The second doctor said she and the baby would be fine, but it would be a high-risk pregnancy. With close monitoring, the pregnancy went well. This child is now eighteen months old and doing fantastic—and so is Mama."
- A grandmother: "Praise the God of life. I have seven children and twenty-seven grands!"
- A husband: "Children are a blessing and changed my life for the better!"

- A wife: "We have three—and none were planned."
- A mom with two teens: "Every life is precious."
- "Life is a gift."
- Dentist dad: "Life—the ultimate gift from God. I choose it and openly accept his gift."
- Future grandparents: "The circle of life—we have four wonderful kids, and in August, we are going to be blessed to be grandparents. God is great!"
- Mom of two kids: "Every life is precious, and motherhood is the best gift God gave me!"
- Mom: "Choose life."
- Dad: "Benefits far outweigh the costs."
- Mom: "Sometimes the most unexpected things in life can be the biggest blessings."
- A mom with two kids: "Being a mother is the best—the most rewarding gift you can receive."
- A mom with her parents: "Ten years ago, I went to Planned Parenthood for birth control and found out I was pregnant. I was offered tissue for crying and three options: abort, adopt, or be a mom. I was twenty-two, single, and had just landed a great job. I knew at that moment that my life, as it was, was over. I chose life. I never looked back. Having my son was the best decision ever. I did not lose my position—and today I still have my job! A baby is a true gift from God."
- A married couple: "We have an adopted daughter—born at two pounds and seven ounces! She is now a twenty-one-year-old college student studying counseling at Moody College!"
- "There is no other choice."
- "We support life!"
- "Thumbs-up for life! Choosing life for your child is a brave, selfless, loving act."

Knights of Columbus Yard Sale

The Knights of Columbus are a large group of Catholic men who provide charitable services and hundreds of different forms. They are known for the Tootsie Roll fund-raisers where men in yellow bibs stand outside high-traffic areas, collect change, and give out candy.

One of our longest-serving members of our council—a military veteran, Boy Scout volunteer, and veteran of hundreds of charity events—shared a story with our project. He said, "My daughter just adopted a baby that a mom gave up: three weeks old, six pounds. I am a very proud grandpa! And my daughter was adopted forty-one years ago."

Here are several more quotes from that day:

- "We are all in this together—choose life."
- "Stay positive."
- Mom: "I was there! I had my boy. Best decision I ever made. I changed my whole life. I made better decisions because I had a child. Be strong. Choose life. Also, parenting isn't for cowards. You will do well."
- Mom and hospital worker involved in births: "I am an ultrasound tech. I had a baby at sixteen. She is now an amazing thirty-six-year-old mother of three. I also adopted two more! One was born addicted (and is) graduating from school this year! I work at Children's Hospital in neonatal unit. Some of those tiny twenty-four-weekers grow up to be 250-pound adults! I know—my cousin is one."
- "You will have a good life."
- "Abortion is not good. That could be someone's child via adoption."
- "I was a state trooper for many years. I have many stories, but just one piece of advice: Choose life."

- Stay strong!
- A wife: "I was adopted. I pray for my birth mother all the time."
- A husband: "And prayer works! I was on the sidewalk at the clinic. Guy walking by calls us stupid, then later, he returns, but we are praying, and he is very quiet."
- "I am a mother of four. I wouldn't change anything in my life."
- A husband: "Some babies who've been aborted—who knows? They could've cured cancer."
- A wife: "We have six grandkids and two great grandkids. Family is the greatest blessing!"

PRC Life Walk

We exhibited at the Life Walk at the Pregnancy Resource Center on Cherry Street in Grand Rapids and were able to get statements from several counselors:

- "God has a plan for you and your baby!"
- "Have your baby—and let your little baby get help!"
- "Breathe."
- "You are not alone! Don't make a decision based on fear. If you walk away today, you still have time. Come to the PRC. We will help you."
- "Choose life."
- "Life is a gift—don't throw it away!"
- "Give the baby a chance. We are here [at PRC] to give you the help you need."
- "Life is precious—there is hope."
- "There are places, like PRC, where their mission is to serve."
- "There is always adoption."

- You can do it. You can make it happen—even if you have no one supporting you, [no] family support, even if [your] family will not help, there are outside agencies willing to help. You are not alone.
- Stop! Slow down. Don't make a decision. Let's talk. Share—call PRC. See where God leads. Please listen.
- When Grandma holds that baby for the first time, she doesn't care about the circumstances around that birth.

I shed a tear with a PRC staff member as she told me her story.

I have been in your shoes. I considered abortion. I am thankful I had information about the long-term effects. I was seventeen. It wasn't easy. I have never regretted my decision, and I have a wonderful twenty-one-year-old son. I chose adoption. He knows me now. It all worked out. He had wonderful parents! At the time, it was like making a decision in the dark—you don't know what will happen.

A staff member was crying and holding her tiny newborn:

Life is a precious gift. I lost one at five and a half months ... having this little guy in my arms ... makes you realize how valuable life really is. We found out this baby was due the second anniversary of the day we buried Isaiah.

Many participants in the walk stopped to thumbprint and share their thoughts.

- A well-known Michigan legislator: "It is a human being—choose life! Being a parent is not always easy, but being a good parent is always worth it."
- "That baby could be a pastor or a teacher—or some other important job in the future."

A woman approached us and apologized for being homeless and shoeless. She told us someone had stolen her shoes. A PRC board member supplied her with an extra pair from her car! The woman said, "My son is four and a half. I was in college and got pregnant. The father did not want to participate—there were paternity tests. My friends and family told me to abort. I don't believe in abortion. I believe all children have the right to life. My son is a sweetie and smart as a whip."

- "Always choose life. You will never regret choosing life."
- "Dios es el camino."

- "You will be glad you kept your baby."
- College student: "Every single life is precious. I did this walk to celebrate this little life that is in me."
- Her friend: "Every life is precious!"
- "There is hope. Seek out wise counsel."
- "Everybody deserves a chance."
- "Choose life."
- "We adopted our youngest! He is a wonderful addition to our life, and we are continuing to be of support to the birth mom!"
- "There is always hope."
- "You can do it!"
- "You are not alone."
- A mom with five kids: "Jesus is Lord."
- A mom with four adopted kids: "We have all been touched by adoption, and we are blessed and thankful for moms who choose life."
- A woman: "Do not fear. Trust in God—even though it seems difficult at the moment. He will bless you."
- A man: "The Lord loves you and your baby so much!"
- "Even though it is tiny, it is a life."
- "Life is precious. I know this is a hard time. Thank you for considering life."
- A mom with her tween-age daughter told us abut what her daughter said at bedtime. "In her prayer, my daughter asked that people would let their babies be born and then they could play with them in their families. My dad was adopted, so I wouldn't be here if his mom hadn't chosen life."
- "Choose life. Jesus is enough."
- "There are people there to help you. Even though the journey might be hard, it is always worth it. Choose life."
- "Always choose life."
- "God will make a way."
- "Seek God."

- "What is conceived is not fearfully, but wonderfully made."
- "This is a gift."
- A mom who made a choice for life: "It is okay to be scared. I did the 'crisis pregnancy' experience, and nine years later, I am still thankful I chose life!"
- A woman in her early thirties: "I am a single mom. This is my son. Fifteen years ago, I was sixteen and pregnant … a lot of emotions happened … then a lot of experiences."
- Grandma added, "And a lot of family help and encouragement. We never turned our back. We made sure no one went without."
- Another mom with a young child: "It worked out. Don't be discouraged. We're lovin' life with a little one!"
- "Every person matters very much to God. The unborn, born … every stage in life, they are all precious to God. I love being a dad. My three amazing children are a blessing, and I love being a grandpa—three times now."
- "Live life."
- "Choose life."
- From a neighbor living next to PRC: "I would like a woman who is pregnant to come here."

The young woman who gave us the following statement was extremely excited about our display. She was overwhelmed with emotion and speechless as she looked it over. We showed her the eight little babies in the clouds that our artist had added, which required looking intently to find them. She seemed dumbfounded and awestruck. All of a sudden, she said, "When I was born, Mom was wearing a blue shirt, picking blueberries that day, so my dad calls me Blueberry. I have had a lot of fruit (blessings) in my life, and I am passing out blessings that God gives me and watching him change the world. Watch God bring his kingdom to earth, with each child he sends here. The kingdom of God resides in us all—even the unborn."

Saint Joseph the Worker's Annual Hispanic Festival

- "Don't give up! Keep your baby alive. My daughter got pregnant while using birth control. She did not expect that! Then, the baby grew outside of the tube, and the doctors expected the baby to die. Today, we were supposed to have a funeral. Instead, we celebrate life! You do not know what will happen!"
- "Always choose life!"
- A mother with her daughter: "Always choose life!"
- A man regarding a life-and-death situation: "Pray on this point!"
- Another man: "He said it all."
- Mom with three small children: "We love family!"
- Three teenage dancers: "You are never alone!"
- "We were born to be real—not to be perfect."
- "Life is too short—smile while you still have teeth."
- "When life gives you one hundred reasons to cry, show life that you have a thousand reasons to smile."

They had more, but I could not write fast enough!

A man and his wife provided me a Spanish version of their comments: "Nosotros estamos ceu la vida! y proteje nios la vida, adelante mujer! No al desa moi."

I showed him the art and how we have religious symbolism throughout, especially the nails. When I gave the nail to him to hold, he raised it above his head and said, "I am honored to touch."

- Five men: "The babies don't ask to come to life—you accept it. You make the decision and will have that decision for the rest of your life! Jesus loves everybody. He does not care if we are old, young—he loves us all."
- Six men: "Quiero vivir. Quiero salir. Quiero nacer. Quiero respire. Quiero vida el mismo salve que tu respires. Sean responsables de los derechos de los ninos."
- "Babies are a blessing that enrich a parent's life."
- A man and wife: "La vida es on grande regalo pero algunas veces hay errores que nunea podras quitar de toda tu vida. NO Abortes y si necesitas ayuda solo tienes que pedirla."
- Dad: "We lost a child to miscarriage, and it affected me such that fifteen years later—now—I am finally getting over the pain of the loss. Can one actually dismiss an abortion without any regret? For me, I believe not."
- A pastor of a nearby Hispanic church: "As an adoptive father, choose adoption! I have two."
- "Love life!"
- Boyfriend: "Choose life!"
- Girlfriend: "We are both pro-life!"
- Dad with three kids: "Ser padre es la mejor vocacion."
- Man and woman: "La vida es bella—sigue adelante blessings!"
- Man, wife, and two kids: "El respeto a la vida."
- "Choose life."
- Woman: "We shall not kill. God brought life into the world. Children are a beautiful gift from God."

- A woman working at the event (regarding the fetus): "It is alive!"
- Another woman working at the event: "It is God's child."
- A female exhibitor: "Trust in Jesus."
- A man: "I have nothing to add. The art said it all."
- "Never give up!"
- Three moms with kids: "Dile si la vida. Todos tenemos derecho a vivir."
- Another woman exhibiting at the event: "Tell your family that you love them today because you do not know when life stops on earth. Faith makes things possible—not easy."
- Man, wife, and child: "Be true to yourself."
- Two young men working at the event: "Choose life."
- Festival visitor: "Life is sacred from the womb to the tomb. There is an option—adoption!"
- A group of firefighters: "Let our actions speak."

IHM Conference

I visited the Immaculate Heart of Mary Church to attend a free conference and listen to Dr. Scott Hahn. It was a wonderful conference, and I got to reconnect with a young man I had not seen since his father's funeral. I had gotten to know Ken Baldwin's family via my wife, and Ken Junior was traveling with Dr. Scott Hahn, a world-renowned Catholic author and speaker!

Dr. Hahn gave a wonderful speech and stayed after the conference to meet with almost everyone who lined up to greet him personally. Although I enjoyed his talk, laughed at the jokes, and nodded at many points, my main goal was to get his thumbprint. I guess I am apologizing after the deed is done. He accommodated me and had to rush to get to his plane. He showed great consideration to everyone, including me. I am very grateful that he added his thumbprint to the art.

In the rush to get this busy man's thumbprint, which he told me at least twice earlier that he did not have time to do this, I used every never-take-no-for-an-answer sales technique I had ever learned on my third request. I waited, last in line, to meet him, but I didn't really want a signature. I just kind of pulled his arm toward the table, put the paint on his thumb, and kind of got 'er done.

I turned my head while he thumb-printed, thanking him immensely as he ran to his waiting car to rush to the airport. When I looked at the tile, his extremely wonderful accommodation to my rude forcefulness resulted in his thumb print being more than two inches outside where I wanted it to be.

In kindergarten crayon language, it was "outside of the lines".

It was my fault. However, I used this miss while instructing more than two thousand of the next participants. I pointed to the obvious out-of-bounds impression, and stated, jokingly, that the guy who did this has a double doctorate—but would you *please* stay within the lines! All of us who instructed participants on where to place their print had too much fun with this. It is ironic that his thumbprint, like his talks and books, could be very instructional. We were able to get the message out to everyone, especially children, that we wanted their thumbprints within the lines!

I was able to secure a couple more prints there and messages

- Mary is pro life, Thank God!
- All life is precious from conception to natural death.

ArtPrize

We spoke to thousands of people at ArtPrize. Many just walked by and did not want to participate. For those who did, many did not have time or preferred not to offer any words. Many wanted the symbolism of their participation to be their words. Of course, several were not happy about our display. ArtPrize was happening during the last few weeks of the election, and those in favor of one party clearly were troubled by our art. Several pro-choice people thumbprinted the art, as they were truly honest "choicers" and were fine with our choice to promote life.

One woman thumbprinted, looked at me, and said, "Except in the case of rape or incest."

Another woman, professionally dressed with a gorgeous scarf and jewelry, wanted to do more than walk by. She took me aside and demanded to know if we were promoting life.

I said, "Yes, this is a very pro-life display."

She began a twenty-minute barrage of complaints about what pro-life people say versus what they do. She railed to me about how we "make" women have their babies and that we do nothing for the kids after they are born. "What about all the kids waiting in foster care for help? Who will pay for food, clothing, and housing?" She named all the standard clichés: men should not be involved in a woman's decision, religion should not be involved in any personal decision of any woman in America where freedom reigns, women need the ability to rule over their own reproductive rights, it is her body and her choice, and on and on and on. She hit every topic ever used to sway women to choice!

When she slowed down, she told me that a young relative was even counseling pregnant women through Planned Parenthood to have third-trimester abortions rather than suffering economic pain or death of the mother.

I told her that I agreed with her on many issues that she brought up. There is a great need for aid to families, and poverty, hunger, and lower economic levels are likely for many women who keep their babies and raise them. I agreed that pro-lifers should do more for the kids already born. I agreed that if a risk to a mother in childbearing could cause her death that drastic action might be necessary, and that some situations require special care, and a one-size-fits-all approach can never be the answer.

We generally agreed about several things she brought up! I don't think that either side argues that more needs to be accomplished for children and families who suffer from poverty or illness.

But when she was done talking, I asked her *the* question: "But are you okay with the process?"

She knew what I was talking about! For those readers who are pro-choice and do not know what a D&E is, please find out. You might then realize why so many choice folks find out what a D&E is and become pro-life forever more.

That was it. She was done with me and left.

Our big event was finally happening. Here are the best of the words of wisdom we received.

- Our first five visitors: "We are all from Traverse City and are very pro-life!"
- A bearded photographer with his mother: "I do not care what you believe. Upon conception, the baby/fetus/embryo has separate DNA—choose adoption."

- His mom: "Ditto what my son said. Choose life!"
- Mom: "When I was sixteen, I got pregnant and had my daughter. I wouldn't change anything in my life."
- Daughter: "I work at my church in Sparta, and I have adopted a set of four siblings!"
- Married couple with two-year-old: "I am looking forward to having a second one—not pushing it out though! But it's worth it!"

In our numerous sessions, I would bang on the steel shin. I noticed that it was quite a good steel drum. The hollow tones changed like a musical instrument depending on where I tapped. It had many different sounds! I decided to allow children to make music with the shin for a minute or two after they thumbprinted. It proved to be a great time for those who participated!

- Two boys: "This was the best day ever!"
- A young mother with a baby in a stroller: "Loving motherhood!"
- The young father: "And fatherhood! A truly awesome experience!"
- Dad with two-year-old son: "Fatherhood is worth it!"
- Man and wife: "I was born in 1961 and adopted! If abortion was legal then, we might not be talking today."
- Two couples: "Choose life! I'm having a grandbaby Norah on Monday September 26, 2016. She will be a princess."
- New grandparents: "Prayers needed for Julienne with Angelman syndrome."
- Man and wife: "Cherish your children!"
- Man and wife: "Choose life! We made it through the childbearing years, and now we have the payback—grandchildren!"
- "Go life!"

- Dad, Mom, and two-year-old: "Regarding family life— it's a blast."
- Mom: "Every child should be a wanted child."
- Mom: "Patience is a virtue."
- Wife of ArtPrize musician: "Celebrate life!"
- Group of five: "Our God is a big God—what is scary to us doesn't matter."
- Dad with two kids under three: "It's the most selfless thing you can do with your life. It's a lot of work. Lot of joy."
- Mom with two kids under three: "There is no greater role than being a parent—and no greater joy than meeting your child."
- Two moms with four kids who banged on the shin: "Kids make a lot of noise."
- A family from India thumbprinted. The dad told me that abortion is illegal there. His wife told me that being a mother is like a "second birth," a new life where your kids are more important than yourself. She told me that it was a waste to not be a mother. I asked if she would write that in her language—and she did.

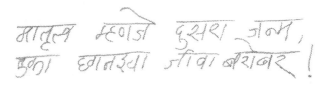

- "We love our grandchildren!"
- Mom with two kids: "I am a teacher and will bring my students to see this display!"
- "Grandmahood is better than motherhood!"
- Dad of three girls: "Your parents run the first half of your left—your kids run the second half!"
- Married couple: "This is fun!"
- Female college student: "You've got this!"
- Four grandmas: "Too cute!"
- Married couple: "It's all about family!"
- Dad of two teen daughters: "If you are unable to raise your child at that time, there are plenty of people who want to adopt!"
- Mom of two girls: "Be steadfast … your mind, your heart. Show more patience than you think you can. The kids won't remember your bad moments, but you will. Best of luck!"
- Mom of two teen boys: "You can do anything you want to do. Never let anyone say you cannot do it. God has your back."
- Mom of teen son and tween daughter: "It's the best adventure you will take! I learn something from them each day."
- Family with four kids under twelve: "Fun day for the kids!"
- Two coworkers at local hospital: "We both work in OB/GYN. It will be all right. Your body knows what to do. Everything will be okay."

One of the women from the hospital was very pregnant, due in March 2017, and she had an ultrasound picture of her baby with its thumb up.

- Mom of adult daughter: "To prospective parents: Calm down. The scary part comes later."
- An event official for the Saint Joseph the Worker's Hispanic Festival: "Reciprocal love and self-gift equal life. Babies are the expression of love and 'living out' the vocation of parenthood!"
- Three moms and three teen daughters: "Loved this!"
- "I taught for many years. A student confided in me about her abortion—and that every year, on that day, she is not happy about her choice."

As people walked by, we would invite them to paint the art. I said, "It costs nothing. We are doing this to promote life."

It was fun to see how people would react and do things like holding their thumbs next to their print on the art for the picture, tell me they did not want to take a picture, or search all over the tiles for just the right spot. We had to push them to print quickly because the paint would dry. I tried to use just the one bottle of paint, which was paid for in the initial $150 that was provided to our artist. She handed me the paint and applicators. We did more than 2,500 prints with that one bottle!

One family came in to print and left their handicapped daughter outside because she could not enter easily. I asked the mom if her daughter would want to thumbprint, and she said yes. I unhooked a few tiles, and we went outside to get her thumbprint! The daughter saw us coming and was very excited that we had thought about her.

I was closing up one night when I saw three moms with strollers and several kids hurrying down the street. I went out to see if they wanted to print. They were exhausted and in a hurry, but they felt the kids would want to do it. I got them all thumbprinted and was showing them the art and telling them about the shin when the moms gasped. I thought I had said something alarming. They told me that their pastor had just given a sermon about the shin and about it being the symbol of God and many other things. They were now unexpectedly next to a ten-foot steel shin!

When ArtPrize was finally over, our crew disassembled and reassembled it at our church in Rockford. It was our fastest dismantle ever, and we did it at night. In the next few days, I was able to show the kids at OLC School the art. I told them about the many Bible verses that were visualized by the art and let them bang on the shin. We moved the art to storage.

We had easily acquired 2,500 thumbprints. The art looked fantastic. Mission accomplished.

The next May the Michigan State council of the Knights of Columbus awarded our council, #7761 their Culture of Life Award at the State Convention on Mackinaw Island.

If you would like to participate in the ArtPeace Project, we can help you make a mosaic to display in your town! Please feel free to email me at pk1776@yahoo.com

CONCLUSION

I have lived a long time and have been involved in the pro-life movement for more than ten years.

I can tell you—whoever you are, wherever you are in the world—that the greatest thing you can do in life is accept your gifts from God. Never look at what happens in your life from an immediate perspective. If you encounter a difficult situation, it can be a blessing. It is easy for us to consider that God has somehow cursed us. If you believe in God, you must realize that God is good, all the time. Trust in God. God has unlimited resources and mercy.

The devil is a liar.

If you can remove emotion, money, and your personal comfort from a decision, would you make a different decision? Do you believe that any suffering you experience can be aligned with the suffering of Jesus? Can you participate in the salvation or the good of all humankind by persevering in tough situations?

This book is more than a book about my trials. It is an urging, a proposition to you, and an enticement to any woman to become a mother. It is encouragement to any man to be a father and to support a mother, especially of your child. A child might be the greatest gift you can give the rest of humankind.

I urge every man and woman of any age to make your choice with these considerations in mind. You will make the best choice of all! God will bless you and bless your children and bless your life.

Thank you.

CONTRIBUTORS

---⋎---

I would like to thank the following people or organizations for supporting or participating in the ArtPeace Project, Isaiah 45:10, or ThumbsUpGR.

- Phyllis Witte, former art instructor, South Christian High School
- Mr. Jim Wisnewski, former art teacher, Catholic Central High School
- Andrea Lucas-Martin, artist
- Palace of India Restaurant, Fulton Street, Grand Rapids Michigan
- Knights of Columbus, Council 7761, Rockford
- Mike Hoxsie
- Jim Nammensma of Ebling & Sons Blacksmiths
- Scott Walcott of Premier Metal Products
- ACE Hardware, Rockford, Michigan
- Our Lady of Consolation Church, Rockford, Michigan
- NUCRAFT Furniture, Michigan
- 40 Days for Life
- Archdiocese of Grand Rapids, Michigan
- Right to Life of Grand Rapids, Michigan
- The Hoxsie family
- Ben Muller Realty and an unknown building owner in 2011
- Janet Weston
- Life International, 72 Ransom, Grand Rapids, Michigan

- Creative Concepts, Rockford, Michigan
- eAgile, Grand Rapids, Michigan
- Roersma and Wurn Builders, Michigan
- Saint Patrick's of Parnell School
- Riverside Christian Reformed, Grand Rapids, Michigan
- Our Lady of Consolation School
- Assumption of the Blessed Virgin Mary Church and School
- Saint Joseph the Worker, Wyoming, Michigan
- Saint Isadore's
- Holy Family Church and School, Caledonia, Michigan
- Baptists for Life
- HELP Pregnancy Crisis Aid, Grand Rapids, Michigan
- South Christian HS, Grand Rapids, Michigan
- West Catholic HS, Grand Rapids, Michigan
- Catholic Central HS, Grand Rapids, Michigan
- Pregnancy Resource Center 415 Cherry St., Grand Rapids, Michigan

ABOUT THE AUTHOR

P J Keeley has been a pro-life advocate for more than ten years. He has been a community outreach volunteer for the 40 Days for Life Grand Rapids, pro-life events chair for Knights of Columbus Council 7761, and has logged thousands of hours at prayer vigils. In addition to being a Knight of Columbus, 3rd Degree, he is a member of Promise-Keepers and a self-taught historian. He is married and has four grown children and lives in West Michigan.

Printed in the United States
By Bookmasters